CRANIAL GUITAR

SELECTED POEMS BY BOB KAUFMAN

INTRODUCTION BY DAVID HENDERSON

EDITED BY GERALD NICOSIA

COFFEE HOUSE PRESS :: MINNEAPOLIS :: 1996

Coffee House Press is supported in part, by a grant provided by the Minnesota State Arts Board, through an appropriation by the Minnesota State Legislature, and by a grant from the National Endowment for the Arts, a federal agency. Additional support has been provided by the Lila Wallace-Reader's Digest Fund; The McKnight Foundation; Lannan Foundation; The Dayton Hudson Foundation; General Mills Foundation; St. Paul Companies; Honeywell Foundation; Star Tribune/Cowles Media Company; Beverly J. and John A. Rollwagen Fund of The Minneapolis Foundation; Prudential Foundation; and The Andrew W. Mellon Foundation.

Coffee House Press books are available to the trade through our primary distributor, Consortium Book Sales & Distribution, 1045 Westgate Drive, Saint Paul, MN 55114. For personal orders, catalogs or other information, write to:
Coffee House Press
27 North Fourth Street, Suite 400, Minneapolis, MN 55401

Library of Congress CIP Data

Kaufman, Bob.
    Cranial guitar : selected poems / by Bob Kaufman ; edited by
  Gerald Nicosia ; introduction by David Henderson.
        p   cm.
    Includes bibliographical references.
    ISBN 1-56689-038-1 (pbk. : alk. paper)
    I. Nicosia, Gerald. II. Title.
PS3561.A84C73   1996   95-31960
811' .54—dc20   CIP

10 9 8 7 6 5 4 3 2

Table of Contents

Selections from
SOLITUDES CROWDED WITH LONELINESS

Selections from
THE ANCIENT RAIN

Uncollected Works

Bibliography

Editor's Note

Editing a posthumous work is always difficult, since the eyes and ears of the writer are not there to test the work against his own memory. But with a writer like Kaufman, the difficulty is multiplied many times. His works were often composed orally in numerous varying versions (as can be seen in sister poems like "Plea" and "Night Sung Sailor's Prayer"), were typeset from transcriptions prepared by others, and then, since he made no effort to save anything, the original manuscripts and galleys were most times lost. The text of *Golden Sardine* is especially suspect, as the early City Lights books were not free of typographical errors, and it is not known who, if anyone, actually corrected the proofs. In editing this volume, with the consultation of Bob's widow, Eileen, I have chosen to retain all the questionable spellings (e.g., megathon), since there is now no way of knowing whether a particular unorthodox spelling is merely a typo, or one of Bob's private coinages. Since Bob was a surrealist, and since surrealists appreciate the intrusion of chance into artistic creation, I can only hope Bob is smiling down from heaven at whatever printer's slips we may now have immortalized as part of his text.

–Gerald Nicosia,
Corte Madera, California, November 29, 1995

INTRODUCTION

Bob Kaufman's life as a poet is unique to American literature. He kept no diary or journal, published no literary essays, wrote no reviews, and maintained no correspondences. He is remembered by three volumes of poetry, and a few broadsides and songs. Up until his death from emphysema in January of 1986, Kaufman was known as a mostly silent, wiry black man who walked the streets of San Francisco's North Beach district day and night often appearing as a mendicant, madman or panhandler.

Yet various schools of American poetry have sung his praises. Recognized early on as a major figure in the Beat Generation of writers and poets, Kaufman is also known as one of America's true surrealist poets, a premier jazz poet, and a major poet of the black consciousness movement. So much did he embody a French tradition of the poet as outsider, madman, and outcast, that in France, Kaufman was called the Black Rimbaud.

Allen Ginsberg, poet: "Simon Watson Taylor, the pataphysician and translator, would make a point every time he went to San Francisco of seeing Kaufman. And I think Kaufman was the only poet that Taylor felt really had a true surrealist muse. As an old habituè of cafe meetings with Breton and the original surrealist groups, he had the taste and knew the real stuff, and knew what it was like in French, too. He was always totally respectful of Kaufman as being the great surrealist American poet."

Jerry Kamstra, writer, cultural activist: "He was actually the man that Herb Caen coined the term 'Beatnik' to describe because he was in the news all the time for being busted. He used to run up and down Grant Avenue jumping on cars and shouting his poetry."

Allen Ginsberg: "He wasn't just political, he was metaphysical, psychological, surrealist, and enlightened in extending his care into the whole society of poetry, seeing that as the revolution. There was a kind of psychological revolution going on along with the liberation of the word."

Jerry Stoll, photographer: "Bob's main concern was the revolution. His poetry was a revolutionary germ that was functioning in people's psyches to transform them. And so I think also that he was always concerned with transforming his own psyche."

Bob Kaufman was born in New Orleans on April 18, 1925. His father, who was half African American and half Jewish, worked for the railroad as a Pullman porter. His mother, a black woman from an old Martinique family, the Vignes, was a schoolteacher. His Jewish surname and Creole-like features were shared with twelve brothers and sisters.

George Kaufman, brother: "There were a lot of clashes and a lot of fun. I think we had a very happy childhood. I would say that our younger days were in the midst of a depression and we didn't realize there was a depression. Our mother was a schoolteacher before she married. She played the piano and I always remember the piano in the living room. She was quite interested in music, the arts, poetry, and I would say that we were born with a book in our hands. Her favorite thing was to go to auctions and buy libraries. We always had tremendous shelves of books all over the house. Possibly this may have been the genesis of Bob's work, from reading at such a young age. The one thing that I regret about this is that my mother died in 1954, before Bob had started writing poetry. She would have been enthralled to read his work, I think. She would have loved it. And she never had a chance to see it. My father was a Pullman porter for the trains that ran between New Orleans and Chicago. We saw him when he was in town, and then he was gone again. And so my mother sort of ran the house, reared the children, trained them in basic values."

According to Kaufman's widow, Eileen Kaufman, Bob's working life began with a job as a cabin boy on the *Henry Gibbons*. Befriended by a first mate who lent him books and helped guide him through his earliest days at sea, Kaufman went on to become a seasoned mate who divided his time on land between New York and San Francisco. It was during this period he became acquainted with some of the nascent Beat Generation figures before the movement was openly declared.

Eventually he was to become one of the major movers in that declaration.

George Kaufman: "Well, Bob and I lived in New York together when he was a seaman. I was a merchant seaman then too. He represented the National Maritime Union at conferences in London and France after the war. Then he got into politics. He was an area director for Henry Wallace's [presidential] campaign in 1948. The Progressive Party. He ran into some real problems. He was an area director in the wrong area and he ran into some real serious problems with the police forces definitely trying to see that his point of view wouldn't be heard in that area of the country. He was arrested many times, brutally treated, thrown into jail cells with no heat and freezing conditions and kept there for a long time. But that never stopped him. He still had his own way of thinking."

Kaufman became well known in both the New York and the West Coast scenes. A jazz aficionado, he was one of the many who used jazz to blur racial and class lines. He came to know and be friends with jazz greats Billie Holiday, Charlie Parker, and many lesser-known musicians and hipsters. And even as he began driving a new Buick and dressing fashionably, he was also becoming known in the black and leftist political communities on both coasts.

Jack Micheline, poet: "We went together and heard Lady Day at the Blackhawk one time in '59. She knew him and talked to him. He gave her some poems written out in longhand, and she took them very gracefully."

Professor Charles Nyland, University of Colorado at Boulder: "For Kaufman jazz seems to have been a force against the destructive. He had some feeling that jazz almost shed a mystical light that enabled one to deal with experiences."

Jerry Stoll met Kaufman in 1956 or 1957 at several of the many poetry readings in San Francisco, when Kaufman's *Abomunist Manifesto* was a big poem on the scene. "Bob was talking about activism. He was functioning as a critic of society in a much more social and political way than any of the other poets in North Beach were. He was a pioneer. I think that it is really clear that people like Ginsberg and the rest of them, when they were political activists, were following Kaufman. They didn't lead Kaufman, he led them. He had the political consciousness."

Stoll introduced Kaufman to his future wife Eileen Singe, a woman of black Irish ancestry who had begun assisting him in his photo shop. Eileen was a legendary beauty of the North Beach scene with long flowing silken black hair, a slender figure, and a dedication to the emerging movement. Kaufman's marriage to Eileen convinced him to give up the itinerant life of a seaman and settle down in San Francisco. He wanted to start a family and be more consistently active in the Beat Generation, a movement that was startlingly radical in the staid 1950s.

In the three year period up until 1960, Kaufman published three broadsides with City Lights Books, run by Lawrence Ferlinghetti, that had published Ginsberg's Beat Generation anthem, "Howl." *Does The Secret Mind Whisper?*, *Abomunist Manifesto*, and *Second April* made Bob Kaufman famous among the Beats. He also became involved in a poet's magazine, *Beatitude*.

Raymond Foye: "*Beatitude* originally was a weekly poetry magazine which Bob Kaufman, William Margolis, John Kelly, and Bernie Uronowicz published at a place called the Bread and Wine Mission, which was a coffeehouse and soup kitchen run by Pierre Delattre in a North Beach neighborhood. It was really meant as a very flexible spontaneous forum for poets to publish their work."

Neeli Cherkovski, poet, biographer: "It was kind of sporadic. They brought out sixteen issues and then it was taken over by City Lights, who did the first *Beatitude Anthology*. "Jail Poems" and *Abomunist Manifesto* are in there. He started this magazine for the community. Kaufman had been a labor organizer and had this idea of the social unit, but it was more like convening. He founded the magazine but he let other people edit it. He didn't take strong editorial control or even that much quality control. It was like, let everybody be a part of it."

Allen Ginsberg: "Bob Kaufman was there on the mimeograph machine doing the actual work of putting out *Beatitude*. I think that was the first time I met him and it was wonderful because I hadn't seen anybody black so much involved in the North Beach poetry scene, adding a kind of enlightened sociability and generosity and contact with all the poets around. And getting it all organized in good taste, earnestness, and energy."

Abomunist Manifesto was put out along with another of Kaufman's popular poems which was sympathetic to Carl Chessman, who was on death row in a California prison. Both works and many others were originally done spontaneously at some of the many Beat Generation poetry readings. It must be remembered that for the Beats, the poetry reading was the national pastime, it was the major event of the day, above and beyond the formal jazz concert or art opening. Kaufman became celebrated for these poems which were not even published until they were well established in the Beat literature which then was still largely unpublished. It was Eileen who insisted her husband help her write them down. Kaufman was really into being a quintessential Beat who cared nothing for publication and who cared everything about spontaneity—about literal beatitude. Kaufman was quintessential in other ways, especially in regard to the Beat Generation's love of nonconformity which was often expressed via the abundant California wine and marijuana, and as it would turn out for him and many others, stronger drink and unusual drugs.

Jerry Stoll: "The community which had been quiet and intimidated by the McCarthy period found an issue, a human rights issue, in the symbolic representation of an individual like Carl Chessman, who was going to be executed. And from that moved into the civil rights struggle very very actively. Bob was ahead of that movement. He was writing his poetry and talking about these kinds of things before the Chessman movement and the Civil Rights movement began."

Amiri Baraka, poet, activist, playwright: "That whole thing about Abomunist, the thing about what Abomunist was . . . Abomination, Abominable . . . and the thing that sounded like communists or something like that. So I had put that together, that he was making some kind of excluded radical, a radical outsider force that he viewed as the Abomunist. And to me the Abomunist was sort of a full-service Beatnik. Let's say pre-commerce. From the real feelings of being opposed to society, and that that whole society had to be overthrown. That's what I got from the publication *Beatitude* and all that writing and *Abomunist Manifesto*."

Tattoo Bob Murphy, poet: "I met Bob at the Coffee Gallery. It was like a weekend night. In North Beach during that time the Beats stayed in on the weekends. They didn't go out because all—what they called—the shams came out. You know, they'd put on beards and strange dress and they'd come down to the Coffee Gallery and the Bagel Shop and they took it over. It was like tourists, but they were phony. So everybody stayed inside. So I decided to be down there one night and Bob was in there. And he was attacking all these people in the Coffee Gallery. And I thought that he was so elegant in the way that he did it. People were buying him drinks as fast as he could say anything. As soon as somebody bought him a drink he would insult them. They had to take it. There was no way they could do anything. I hooked up with him then. I said this is a person that's after my own heart, because that's how I felt about these people too. I could see it. He displayed it to me. I saw myself potentially as being one of these people down there on Friday night, and I didn't want to be one of these people."

Nineteen-fifty-nine was the biggest year for Kaufman. Eileen gave birth to a son whom they named Parker, after the legendary jazzman, Charlie Parker. And Bob's first book, *Solitudes Crowded with Loneliness* was published by the distinguished poetry press New Directions. He had begun work on a novel and a play, *The Matchbox*, and had become something of a political leader as well.

Jerry Kamstra: "We had a big demonstration once, in about 1959, because the cops were busting all the hotels for marijuana. I had a bookstore on Grant Avenue. I organized a big protest meeting one Saturday and made a bunch of picket signs and rented a P.A. system. Saturday morning at ten o' clock in Washington Square there were 200 people out there and we were all talking about police harassment. And I remember when Bob Kaufman began to speak the bells of St. Peter and Paul's began to toll. And he spoke right through and between it, it was great poetry.

Raymond Foye: "At that point he was interested in seeing his work in print and communicating and reading. But the results that ensued were dire. I mean, he was targeted by the police as a subversive. He was arrested thirty-six times in one year. Bob Kaufman and the great French poet Villon have one thing in common which is that when the scholars write their biographies they're gonna have to go back to the police records. Bob really paid dearly for a lot of the positions he took at that time in his poetry and in his lifestyle." The Coexistence Bagel Shop was the nerve center for the emerging Beat. The police would often stop in and harass the patrons. Foye continues, "Bob had placed a surrealist text (*Olé,* by Bill Margolis) in the window in which he said that Hitler was reincarnated and was back in San Francisco and his name was Bigarani, the police officer whose beat was North Beach. He came into the Bagel Shop and took it down."

Paul Landry, poet: "Bigarani, yeah, he had a real hatred for Beatniks. He went into the Coexistence Bagel Shop and tore some poetry off the board there. Bob just stood up and pissed on the guy's pants. He was talking to him, and while he was talking to him he took it out and peed on the guy, you know. Bigarani looked down and saw what it was and they took him off. And from what I understand they 'iceboxed' him for about a month. What they would do is they'd put him in long enough in one place and you'd go down there with your money to get him out and they'd hustle him off to some other place, and they put him in jails all over the city and keep him circulating until finally you could get into the system far enough to get him back out. At that time wherever you went there was a 'Bob Kaufman Can' by the door that you put your nickels and dimes and quarters in because Bob was constantly in jail and you were constantly bailing him out. "

Eileen Kaufman: "They were trying to put Bob in jail for drunk and disorderly every time they saw him on the street. They didn't like it when he hopped up on tables and spouted poetry. They were against us from the git-go. We were one of the first blatant interracial couples in North Beach that stayed together and had children. So they were afraid of a pattern there. And they got so mad at Bob they would stop the elevators between floors and beat him up."

Raymond Foye: "Around 1960 . . . Bob was spending so much time in jail being beaten by police that finally he decided to get out of there."

Allen Ginsberg: "It was part of a larger scale move to exploit the literary notoriety of North Beach. Drive out all the literary people and the poets and install topless sideshows for tourists."

Raymond Foye: "North Beach is a very small community in many ways and Bob pretty much had to get out of the scene for a while. He was up for the Guinness Poetry Prize and was asked to read at Harvard University. They sent him a plane ticket."

Eileen Kaufman: "We went on to New York and lived in the Village and the East Village off and on for about three years. Bob was supposed to read at Harvard, but he was not in any condition to read. He was taking speed because he was drinking and didn't want to drink. But that didn't cure his drinking. It was much worse because it was a psychological addiction as well as physical. So he didn't read at Harvard that year. But he had a lot of readings in John Mitchell's little cafe, the Gaslight. And he used to read at other Village places, such as the Fat Black Pussy Cat, and Café Wha."

Ted Joans, poet, early Greenwich Village Beat: "The cat knocked on the door and I opened the door and there was a black cat standing there with a chick who has a little baby. I said, 'Yes?' 'Allen [Ginsberg] told me I could come over and stay at your pad.' I said, 'No, I don't know, man; what's your name?' 'My name is Bob, man.' 'Bob who?' 'Bob Kaufman.' I said, 'No, Allen told me that he would send someone over now and then.' He said, 'Bob Kaufman, the poet.' I said, 'I thought you were white, man.' Really, 'cause I used to see the name. I'd read the cat's name. But I just thought, Bob Kaufman, Allen Ginsberg. You know, all those cats with those Jewish names. The same thing."

Joe Overstreet, painter: "I had moved to Fifth street. 629 East Fifth street. I was walking down Fifth street between First and Avenue A. At the time some of the tenements were being torn down for co-ops that are there now. It was January or February and it was real cold. There was snow on the ground. I had left the Cedar Street Bar. It was about three-thirty, four in the morning. I passed this building and I heard a whimper. At first I thought it was an animal. I heard it again. It was a faint cry. I walked down some steps to the basement and saw a faint candlelight back there. I could see this small bundle around this baby. I could see the baby's face and it was Parker. Bob had moved into this abandoned building with Parker. All he had was a blanket or something around the baby. It wasn't freezing, he had enough covers and so forth. But the baby was obviously very cold. I picked up the baby and got Bob up. And I took the baby to my house for just a week or two until Eileen returned from San Francisco. Well, Eileen came back with money. They got a place on Second Street in a building where Allen Ginsberg had an apartment."

Allen Ginsberg: "I had an apartment at 170 East Second Street. They got an apartment upstairs, so we were neighbors for about a year, I think. Herbert Huncke also had an apartment upstairs for a while. We were visited one great day by Timothy Leary. Leary had been experimenting with psilocybin at Harvard, at the Center for the Study of the Human Personality, or something. And he arranged to visit New York and stay at my apartment for a day. And Kerouac came in and Bob Kaufman also from upstairs. Jack and Bob both took psilocybin. That was the time when Jack looked out the window and said, 'Walking on water wasn't built in a day,' in appreciation of this strange advance in chemistry. Bob was sitting in the bed and was very high on the psilocybin. It may have been his first time—I'm not sure—for a psychedelic. I hadn't taken anything. I was the stabilizer in my apartment. He was tripping. I don't know if it was bumcake or fear or troubled or cosmic apprehension. He wanted some kind of reassurance—historical, cosmic, reassurance. What was going to happen to earth?—which was always on our minds, all of us, whenever we got high then—a feeling that we were somewhat responsible for directing the course of human destiny. Or having had the experience of a large mind we should at least say a word or put a spirit into things."

Raymond Foye: "After a couple of years in New York, Eileen, who was here with Parker, finally had had enough. She had found a ride back to San Francisco. She arranged for her and Parker and Bob to drive back that afternoon. And Bob was on his way to meet them to catch this ride back to North Beach and he was walking through Washington Square Park and a police woman arrested him for walking on the grass. He was sent to the Tombs first, then he was sent to Riker's Island, and then to Bellevue Hospital where he was termed a behavioral problem and given involuntary shock treatment."

John Fiske, sound engineer, East Village figure: "Somewhere the authorities shaved his head. And this was traumatic to him. The first time that I interacted with him I had just had my own head shaved and it was right at that period I met him in Washington Square Park. His hand motions, which were erratic, seemed to be writing. In his silence he seemed to be writing. He was at that time not articulate. He mumbled a great deal. But then his hand motions seemed to be intended to communicate to the cosmos. It wasn't as though he was communicating to an individual."

Eileen Kaufman: "It was the next fall, October, November. Lawrence [Ferlinghetti] and Allen [Ginsberg] and I found out where he was—with Alex Trocchi—and sent him airfare to get back here in a hurry. So he came in about a week before Kennedy was shot. It was so beautiful. He was so great. We were having such a good time. We were looking over old poems for *Solitudes* before the Kennedy thing. And then he saw it on television and just went to pieces. After that happened he didn't speak in any lengthy sentences or anything. He might say 'Hi' or 'You got a cigarette?' or something like that. But he really never started to elucidate until the Vietnam War ended."

Raymond Foye: "Bob had actually met President Kennedy in San Francisco on a campaign swing, and he loved him a great deal. He felt that there was real hope with someone like Kennedy in the White House. When Kennedy was shot, he made a statement to Eileen to the effect that when a president is killed things have gone too far. That assassination prompted a number of horrific visions, and he felt that the only appropriate response at that point was to take a Buddhist vow of silence. Which is what he did. He ceased to speak or write. Bob always considered himself a Buddhist. He said this quite a few times. That was his religious faith. I think in Bob's mind there was a very clear equation between the priesthood and being a poet. He felt that it was a calling to a higher order. It involved a vow of poverty, it involved devotion to nonmaterialistic values, and it really meant putting yourself at the service of a higher power, be it inspirational or the holy spirit. And moreover he believed that these aspects of divinity were present at all times and that they were accessible to all of us. But he, as a poet, was there to channel these forces."

Kaufman's Buddhist vow of silence had a great impact upon all who came in contact with him, especially the younger poets. It made him a figure of great mystery, and added to the near legendary status he had already attained.

Tattoo Bob Murphy: "Bob was right next to me and I didn't know he was there. He was into this Buddhist seclusion period where he didn't go out. I was downstairs haggling with the landlord one day and down the stairs comes Bob in this red, really red, bathrobe. A short bathrobe with no pants and no shoes and socks. He's going for a Coke. I hid behind the Coke machine and said, 'Hey, shit man, that shit will kill you—let's go grab a burgie.' And he looked up and recognized me. I'd been living next door to him for a year and didn't even know it.

"The room sounded like rain coming down. It always sounded like rain. It was a fan or something. I think that's where he got that idea for 'Ancient Rain.'

"When I'd be in Bob's room we never talked to each other. I'd be on the bed and he'd be laying back on the bed on a pillow with his hands behind his head. We communicated like in silence. There was an old plastic curtain on the window and then a wall right there. You couldn't see anything out the window except the wall. Every once in a while the wind would blow this old plastic curtain. It was all torn and the room was a shambles anyway. And that was the form. Like, okay, we know we're here. We know that there is something that's here between us. We didn't have to talk. He didn't just jam completely and shut off. He could have done that. He could have remained silent for the rest of his life."

In 1973, just after the Vietnam War ended, Bob and Eileen Kaufman were in Palo Alto with a group of friends attending an exhibition of photographs before visiting Kenneth Patchen's widow, Miriam. Eileen Kaufman recalls, "There was a little chamber group playing. I was talking to some people and all of a sudden Bob began to recite "Murder in the Cathedral," by Eliot. And that was the first thing he said when he came out of his silence. And people were just startled, they had their cups halfway to their mouths. They hadn't heard him for years and years and he started just like that. And he said to me: 'All those ships that never sailed/Today I bring them home and let them sail forever.' The most beautiful poem. I didn't even know he was working on it. But from then on he was very lucid. I never gave up on Bob. I knew he'd surprise us all one day and come out and be as beautiful as ever."

Bob began reading again, mainly at Malvina's, a poet's coffeehouse on upper Grant Avenue, up from Washington Square and St. Peter and Paul's Church. He also read often at the Intersection, a poet's theater, in a church also in North Beach.

Parker Kaufman, son: "We were staying together in San Rafael on Canal Street in an apartment complex. That was the longest we stayed together that I was able to remember. I understand we were all living together when I was a baby, but I don't have any memory of that. But he stayed with us for about eight months. It was interesting because I didn't really have a father most of my life and all of a sudden I do. He was taking total command of my life: 'You can't do this, you can't do that.' But it worked out. It was all right. I rebelled against it, of course. I think everybody would. But we worked it out. We got buddy-buddy. We were watching football games together and rooting for opposite teams: 'You wanna bet?'—you know. And it was fun. It was my mom and me and him and it was great. I wish it could have continued, but his health got worse and he had to go into some kind of hospital or something.

"I was joining the baseball league and I didn't have anybody to practice with except for when the team practiced. So I remember one day I said, 'I'm gonna go to the park and see if I can find somebody to practice with.' And he goes, 'Well, I'll hit you some balls.' So we went up to the park. He took about thirty-five swings before he finally got one out to me. By that time I was practically sitting down on the grass and all of a sudden this ball comes lofting out to me. I said, 'Oh my god, he hit the ball to me.' After that he started hitting them pretty regularly. It was a good session. It lasted about three-and-a-half hours."

Jean Carlisle, North Beach photographer: "Bob had been living with Eileen and Parker in Marin County, and something happened where he was no longer welcome to live there. He ended up living on a floor in a storefront of Kush's Cloud House. And Bob was ill. He had bronchitis going into pneumonia. One afternoon Alix Geluardi called me and said Bob was sick. 'I wish we could find him somewhere to live.' I said, 'Well, I have a big flat and perhaps I could accommodate him.' The next thing I knew I had Bob. Bob lived with us for two months. Just a couple of nights before he came to us he had gone on a binge in North Beach and had fallen off the pier at three-thirty in the morning and lost his teeth and his glasses and his hearing aid all at once."

Raymond Foye: "Bob was living in a fleabag hotel on the corner of Broadway and Columbus Avenue. Early one morning a fire swept through that hotel and Bob was left homeless. I saw him that morning looking a little bit shaken. He mumbled something about having just survived Dante's Inferno. I didn't know quite what he meant. I thought it was just another flight of fancy. As I walked down the street I saw that this hotel had pretty much completely burned down. Later that afternoon, after the fire had been put out and the firemen left, I snuck into the hotel. I knew where Bob's room was. Although people had said he had stopped writing years ago I knew that that probably wasn't the case. It's very hard for a creative artist as intense as Bob Kaufman to really stop writing. So I went in to the hotel. I climbed over the police lines and snuck in there and went up to his room. The room was nothing more than a pile of charcoal. But at the bottom of this pile of burnt-out wood and rubble I found this famous Moroccan leather binder which contained his poems. The poems were singed around the edges, but I carried them out and brought them over to City Lights' publishing office, over the bookstore on the second floor. We carefully peeled these manuscript pages off, one by one. They were soaked with water from the fire hoses. We laid them out all around the office. Looking at these extraordinary handwritten poems I remember Ferlinghetti was there just beside himself. He couldn't believe what we were seeing. It was like opening King Tut's Tomb for the first time and seeing all these extraordinary relics. So we realized at that point that Bob had still been writing. And that really became the core of *The Ancient Rain*."

Lynne Wildey, poet, student, became involved with Bob Kaufman: "He lived alone. He said he was lonely. He didn't want to be alone anymore, and he asked me to come and stay with him. Life began again with the new person and the new family. He hadn't been in a family way in years. . . . I think for the first year-and-an-half I was in total awe of him. And of course there was the vast difference in our ages. He was twenty-two years older than me. That gap takes a lot of understanding, silent understanding to begin to understand who is this person, where is this person coming from.

"We had a radio when we moved into this little hotel in North Beach. There was no window. There was no heat because there was a rent strike in the hotel that winter. We used to play jazz twenty-four hours a day. The radio never got turned off. We'd stay in the bed to get warm sometimes, or I'd wrap blankets around him. He'd write in the cold under piles of blankets. He wasn't too well then. But the objects that were there, beyond the bare requirements of human necessity, were there for poetry. So the room, in itself, had a habitation that was not necessarily of the material world. People were aware of this and people were aware of the poetry in the room. Sometimes we'd have thirteen people in a room barely larger than a bed. People sitting on top of each other in the corners. Eight people on the bed. [Jack] Micheline and Bob screaming poems at each other all night. People came into the room, it was for poetry. People we knew from the drug underworld would stop by just to say hello for the experience."

Kaufman had his admirers, but he also had his detractors. Specs, the proprietor of the bar of the same name—across Columbus Avenue from Vesuvio's—regarded Kaufman as a freeloader who never worked a day in his life. Since Specs was an avid seaman—his claim to fame was having been lost at sea and rescued after a terrific storm off of San Francisco—one would think that he and Kaufman would have had a lot in common. But Kaufman was known to carry on in his place. One incident involved Kaufman and Wildey leaving many rounds of drinks and beers on Spec's bar and going across to Vesuvio's and ordering more rounds there, forgetting about the bill at Spec's. He had been accustomed to Kaufman often not having the money for a drink or cigarettes, but this time he had more than enough money. This episode got Spec's goat to the extent that he eighty-sixed Kaufman and Wildey from his bar.

This episode occurred soon after Kaufman received a $12,500 grant from the National Endowment for the Arts. Raymond Foye, who was most responsible for getting him this windfall, figured it was the most money Bob had probably ever had at one time in his life. That might be true certainly about his life as a Beatnik, but who could know of his entire life? It was known that when Kaufman was a seaman he often owned brand new cars. And seamen were known to accumulate large sums of money, since they spent long periods of time at sea.

Kaufman was often eighty-sixed from the bars of North Beach for one reason or another, which was not easy to do in those traditionally hard-drinking bars, but Kaufman was in the top ten every year. It had to be a mark of distinction, dubious as it may sound, to so disturb the hard edge of these old seaman, roustabout, and stevedore bars, Broadway hustler joints and way-back beatnik/biker vortices—all havens for every kind of wild character imaginable. Kaufman's string of eighty-sixes may well have been some kind of Zen trick that he exercised upon frequent occasion to test boundaries, to keep the faith of the extreme.

Kaufman's reemergence also had a lot to do with Q.R. Hand, a poet, community health activist and Mission District sage. "Bob was constantly, constantly sick. He wasn't paying attention to anything. He hadn't gotten his hearing aid, and his eyes needed glasses. So there's no telling how much of his being out there on his own someplace else seemingly crazy was attributable to him actually seeing and hearing and being disoriented in a way."

Hand had Kaufman undergo a medical and dental examination that eventually resulted in new glasses, a new hearing aid, and a new set of false teeth. Suddenly Kaufman was wholly in the world again. But it was almost as if he had to relearn how to talk. His voice sounded raspy, almost like Miles Davis's voice; sandy, with a bit of white noise in there. The decline of his hearing may have contributed to a loss of pitch in his tone, but there was still the wry, raspy, light baritone he had in the fifties, always melodic, spaced by jazz-like intervals of silence.

Lynn Wildey: "It got so Bob couldn't stay in North Beach. We needed to leave because Bob was getting ill. We went to live in the Redwoods for nine months."

Kaufman and Wildey eventually returned to San Francisco, but not to the single-room-occupancy hotels of North Beach. They lived at a number of residences in the Mission District before settling in a two story cottage in the largely black section of Bayview, which bordered on Hunters Point, the black residential stronghold. Both areas were effectively separated from the city by the elevated Bayshore Freeway.

North Beach was still the poetry capital of California as the Beat Generation became the flower power/love generation. But as the Beats dispersed, the multicultural Mission District became the poetry focus of San Francisco. Bob Kaufman was a part of that transition. North Beach, which was becoming more and more an extension of the adjacent Chinatown, became much more exclusive than the wide-open Mission District, where the rents were cheaper and there was an endless array of joints and venues for poetry scenes. And also with the largely gay Castro District adjacent and the emerging hip South-of-Market District within walking distance, and Haight-Ashbury just a short ride over the Twin Peaks—the Mission District was more centrally located than North Beach. The Western Addition Cultural Center had remained the lone black arts institution in the Western-Addition/Fillmore district, which had been largely black until the advent of Bill Graham's hippy dances at the Fillmore Ballroom. So Kaufman and Wildey became a presence at a wider range of parties, events, poetry readings, and music concerts than his existence in North Beach had afforded him.

It was important to have a celebrated black poet in the San Francisco community for such a long time. Kaufman had long been essential to a black literary tradition in San Francisco that included, among others, Ishmael Reed, Maya Angelou, Ernest Gaines, Conyus Calhoun, Reginald Lockett, Reggie Majors, and his daughter Devorah.

Kaufman had been there when the Beats began that psychic birthing pain that broke a lot of heads through into a new reality, a reality that did not just renounce conformity, but offered alternatives: jazz instead of European classical music; grass and psychedelics instead of hard alcohol; communal living, natural foods, vegetarianism, and Buddhism (and an appreciation of other religions) instead of Christianity; and a lack of racial antagonism by demonstrating relationships that crossed racial lines. Many early Beats were jazz hipsters who united around jazz in multiracial relationships. Kaufman is only the tip of the iceberg of the many blacks involved in the Beat Generation—most of whom have gone unsung. But Mardou Fox as Kerouac's portrait of a black woman in his novel *The Subterraneans*, or John Cassavetes in his film *Shadows* show close and even intimate interracial relationships of that time, the mid to late 1950s.

But Kaufman went beyond a Rimbaud-type poetic existence and lived true to the tradition he had perceived. He went to the end of dope, to the end of institutional outpatient insanity, to the end of alcohol, and to the end of poetry. And it was recognized that he had achieved a high level of perfection and mastery of the art of poetry, which gained him the respect and devotion of all who read his work. He became a devotional figure to many of the younger poets, and a living legend to the black poets who knew that he had been a favorite of Langston Hughes, appearing in virtually all of the great African American poet-mentor's several anthologies of black poetry.

Kaufman was small in size, but to confront him was to recognize another order of measurement. He generated a power not of stature, but of dedication, a dedication to poetry, a dedication to suffering— not that he thought them one and the same. But he was not afraid of suffering. But to see him you knew at once he was not bullshitting.

There was not a false move on the man. He had prepared himself to go all the way, whether it be through poetry or jazz or his special mode of Buddhism, a Buddhism merged with an African American mysticism totally unique to and in synch with New Age California.

Raymond Foye: "Bob Kaufman had a tremendously wide knowledge of poetry, and his approach to poetry was really in keeping with poetry as an oral art. I mean, it doesn't come out of writing, it comes out of speech and recitation. There is an old saying that 'thought is formed in the mouth.' Bob had this knowledge of American poetry he could call on at will and endlessly recite from Eliot, Charles Olson, Stephen Spender, Claude McKay, or Langston Hughes for hours on end. And he would often times mix these poems in with his own poems so you didn't know where Eliot left off and where Bob Kaufman began. And that was not an egotistical way of putting himself on that level, it simply had to do with the fact that for Bob all poetry was one. There was a commonality to poetry in his mind and it's why later in life he wrote poems and never signed his name, often times leaving them behind in cafes—he'd write something on a napkin and leave it behind. And things were often lost, thrown away."

In the eighties Kaufman would read at a poetry reading now and then. In bars or at parties or in parks he would often recite from "Murder in the Cathedral" or "The Waste Land" by Eliot, or from other poets he admired. Or he would recite pieces from his own poetry, but never by title, only passages that would have a strange resonance with what was going on in the room, the city, the nation, or beyond. And then he would often drift back into his spontaneous poetry.

He once yelled at poet Gary Gach in a cafe on Columbus Avenue across from the Pagoda Theater and St. Peter and Paul's church regarding a crisis in Arab-Israeli relations:

"THE WAILING WALL IS ON THE ROCKS!"

"THE WAILING WALL IS ON THE ROCKS!"

Nate Mackey, professor at the University of California, Santa Cruz: "There was a part of him that certainly resisted careerist moves. He wasn't somebody trying to ensure his place in the Norton Poetry Anthology or trying to make sure he got onto the syllabi of poetry courses in universities. He didn't do a whole lot of readings at universities. The thing that he's remembered as and revered as is as a street poet, and that's diametrically opposed to the kinds of institutionalizations of the poet. He in many ways resisted that. That was contrary to really being a poet for him, to go after that kind of recognition and to make one's self available to public consumption. Much of what people pass on in stories about him are anecdotes about his outrageousness, and that was an integral part of his understanding of what being a poet was. And in many ways the relative obscurity that his work has remained in is consistent with and is an outgrowth of that. He was not out there trying to make it."

Kaufman's lyric, "Green, Green Rocky Road," was transcribed and written up as song lyrics by Len Chandler from a few sessions with Kaufman. Later, Chandler expressed confusion about the writer's credits not being attributed to Kaufman by the various artists who recorded the song, including The New Christy Minstrels and Peter, Paul and Mary, who have the song listed as "traditional" on their recordings. Kaufman received no remuneration for his song. Jazz composer Steve Lacy also used a Kaufman poem on one of his L.P.s, but attributed the lack of payment to Kaufman as a problem of the international music publishers. He took no personal responsibility for Kaufman being remunerated. Neither did Peter, Paul and Mary.

When Lynn Wildey and Bob Kaufman came together, Kaufman was established quite differently from his earlier years. For one, he had fame, which is different from being the rising star of a new movement. That movement had become established as the Beat Generation. It was a fact, it was part of history. When they came together in the eighties, Bob had endured the worst of the experiences that could well be termed "tragic." And though he still bore ravages of his experiences, as he writes about in, "Would You Wear My Eyes," he had survived. And he had remained in San Francisco, along with Ferlinghetti, Lamantia, Rexroth, Oppen, and Patchen, forming a wonderfully unusual pantheon of American poetry.

Because of Wildey's late but intense involvement with higher education, she thought of Bob as a teacher as well as a companion. As she says, she was often in awe of him. A lot of this had to do with Kaufman's fame, which was a fame of trueness, of dedication, and of consistency. He was a poet on the scene, like a seaman at his station. He had that sea gaze of the long journey with no fear.

And because Wildey was from "the street" as well, and could party as hard as anyone, she also had that respect for poetry that is closer to the love of a working class person for poetry, for the poet, or for any person who had achieved a distinction, but still lived among and was accessible to them.

Lynn Wildey: "Bob kept it going. He always had something moving, so the consciousness would be acute—but he kept the beat, the rhythm. He would tell stories with very few words. He was into exploring the nature of consciousness. He loved poets. He would jump up and scream, take charge of a room. If people were getting square he'd jump up and swirl around. When he would walk into a room people would stop saying mundane things and be unusual . . . they would say things they'd never say . . . they'd bring you to the peak experiences of their lives. He was a hardworking man, very tensile. He looked frail but he could pull off some very amazing physical feats."

Wildey said Kaufman saw sound as sculpture, and often referred to him as a sound poet. He would lie in bed and talk to himself in mantra-like rhythms. He would sound out a poem over and over to her in a bar room corner. She would snap her fingers in the way Kaufman would do, with a fast meter and clusters of rhythms and with the angled way he moved his arms up and down and held his chest forward. "He could do magical things with sound," Wildey remembers, "he sat up all night mouthing sounds into the night." He taught her a mantra and an accompanying rhythm that would make strange things happen. With his fingers, he could summon something called an "electronic" being. It was ectoplasmic and hovered in the room. Once they were doing the mantra and someone began pounding on the door shouting "I am a demon and I know you're doing a mantra in there." The rhythm alone would cause people to drop things—things to fall, people to act strangely.

Wildey collected poems Kaufman wrote up until the time of his death. Some she copied from the "sounding" out of lines he worked on in his mind. Wildey, at the end of Kaufman's life, sought to preserve what she could of his last days. Before he entered the hospital for the last time, they visited the Zen Center. He appreciated Philip Whalen and his mediation between his poetry and Buddhist practice.

In 1986, just after his death, Wildey said, "He was supposed to have died two-and-a-half years ago—medically it was a miracle."

Lawrence Ferlinghetti, poet: "The society systematically murders the poet, decimates the subjective in everyone. Materialist society, the capitalist economy, that's what it does. The State aids and abets that process. The subjective is constantly under attack. So the position of Bob Kaufman is the classic position. The only valid position for a poet these days is like a bearer of Eros, the personification of the truly free individual, the position of the poet as enemy of the state, which I consider an admirable position for an artist or a poet. And the only valid one, as I said before, in the face of the continual attack on the freedom of the individual and his subjectivity. Bob was a sacrificial victim in the sense that there was no compromise with him. He couldn't live any other way but the way he lived.

"After his cremation they paraded up and down Grant Avenue with the New Orleans marching band. They paraded down to the Marina Green and there were three boats. One with the press on it, one with Bob's relatives, and one with the poets. And they went out into the middle of the bay and scattered his ashes. It happened that when the boats came back into the dock and the poets got off the boat and they were just standing by the dockside, a huge rainbow appeared in the sky, across the whole bay."

One of the few persons to really take on Kaufman's poetry in the English language was a professor at the University of Colorado at Boulder, Dr. Charles Nyland. "Actually, we could say the speech is beautiful. It has jazz elements, there's improvisation. The rhetoric is stylized, actually, but that pattern permits him to combine images with a logic that is a surrealistic logic. This is a mode, I suppose, that had considerable appeal not only to Kaufman, but to a good number of the Beat poets. André Breton called Ted Joans a surrealist, and Joans spoke of Kaufman as being a surrealist. His surrealism is not Breton's automatic writing. It appears to be logically derived from his awareness of paradox and discontinuity and from experimenting with bebop and black speech patterns. And in discovering in them a means, a vehicle, to carry his vision, and a means that gives him a certain aesthetic distance when he makes use of personal experiences. Some of Kaufman's experiences were horrible. Some of his experiences in a way detracted from his human dignity. And yet he was able to utilize these in such a way that the meaning that is derived from them is aesthetically satisfying and contributes to wisdom."

Jack Micheline: "He knew how to rumble. He knew how to live it. He lived it quick. He lived it fast. He was a real poet. How many real poets can you meet in your life? He was close to what was happening and he was out of it. He was into some magic of his own. He had magic. The man was a magician. He had beautiful magic."

—David Henderson

Note: Most of the quotations in this piece are taken from the National Public Radio documentary written and produced by David Henderson, with Vic Bedoian co-producer, entitled, "Bob Kaufman, Poet." The documentary was sponsored by the California Council for the Humanities, the Zellerbach Family Fund of San Francisco, the National Endowment for the Arts, Moe's Bookstore, Cody's Books, City Lights Bookstore, and the Pacifica Foundation. The two-hour documentary was first aired on KPFA-FM in Berkeley in April of 1991.

GOLDEN SARDINE

CARL CHESSMAN INTERVIEWS THE P.T.A. IN
HIS SWANK GAS CHAMBER BEFORE LEAVING
ON HIS ANNUAL INSPECTION OF CAPITAL,
TOUR OF NORTHERN CALIFORNIA DEATH
UNIVERSITIES, HAPPY.

Carl Chessman is in sickly California writing death threats to the
Wizard of Oz, his trial is being held in the stomach of Junipero
Serra, at last the game starts, chessman steals all the bases & returns
to his tomb to receive the last sacraments from Shirley Temple.

Silence, oyegas, oyegas, f.ms, the corpsey bailiff, atones, ready. ALL
STAND, AL HITCHCOCK PRESENTS, CARL CHESSMAN OF THE
UNIVERSE OF CALIFORNIA VS. THE PEOPLE'S GODLY GAS
BIRTHRIGHT.

chessman draws an impressionistic picture of vinnie van go with
three beautiful stink flowers stuffed into his vacant ear, declares
mothers' day out of bounds for spacemen, discusses cute gas stove
being put in the game room by the gold star mothers, feels their
meters, pronounces them queer, & offers to slap their bosoms into
exotic shapes without charge, free.

Chessman names the last week in December national week.
offered Jesus free room & board.

CARL CHESSMAN KNOWS, THE GOVERNOR OF CALIFORNIA
KNOWS, GOOD JOHNNY THE POPE KNOWS, SALVATORE AGRON
KNOWS & ALL THE LEAKY EYED POETS KNOW, IN THEIR PORES,
NO ONE IS GUILTY OF ANYTHING AT ANY TIME ANYWHERE IN
ANYPLACE, ASK THOSE HEBREW ECSTATICS UP THERE ON THE
TREES OF SORROW, MYSTIC BLOODFRUIT PICKED IN THE SEA-
SON OF THE DAMNED, LIVE FROM THE AMAZON, THE MARTYRS'

DAUGHTER . . . . FOUR MIDWESTERN SAINTS, GIVE HEADS
. . . RATHER THEMSELVES TO LUSTY, PAGAN, RAW, CLOTHING-
LESS JIVARO TEENAGER, SWEETHEART OF THE YOUNG HEAD-
HUNTER.

CHESSMAN CALLS UP GOD, WANTS TO KNOW AT ONCE, DOES
SANTA CLAUS BELIEVE IN CHILDREN? GOD GETS PANICKY &
PUTS DOWN HIS GUITAR, BEGINS TO MAKE GREAT SIMULTANE-
OUS PHONE CALLS TO EVERYONE HE CAN THINK OF & IS GIV-
ING OUT UNTRUE ADDRESSES UNTIL CHESSMAN ACCUSES HIM
OF FELONIOUS DEISM, GOD COPS OUT & GIVES CHESSMAN A
LITTLE RED DEW LINE TELEPHONE, GOD ACCUSES CHESSMAN
OF . . . . BEING GOD, CHESSMAN DENIES EVER HAVING BEEN
GOD, REMINDS GOD OF THEIR DUSTBOWLING YEARS, CHESS-
MAN WINS WEEKEND PASS TO HOME FOR UNWED STEPMOTH-
ERS, & WINS VILLAGE HORSESHOE CONTEST,

chessman announces new butane concept of humility, chess is
going around lifting skirts of manacled altar boys at religious
monastery of deliberate unsexual design,

now old curveballer carl, great san quentin on mangashouse
gang is going to throw out the first president of the season, old
carl tells an anecdote about god's wild youth.

This is a poem about a
nobody, twenty something
years old, whose parents
sent him to a good college
but, who instead read buddhist
magazines & of course became god,
he is now standing in front of his
parents' house saying, they think I've been in school for four years,
how can i walk in cold and tell them i am god, i think i'll go over
to chessman's little studio & sleep.

Now the march of the wire sculpture poets in old collector carl's san quentin word saloon, cool wind litanies, as they unwrap their image patches, surrealist post card day at carl's & now the poets fearlessly unscrew their heads, & carl sketches their brain in the nude . . . . & now carl long distance chessman gets a call from a leper colony that wants his autograph, carl flies to the leper nation in his indian aeroplane & signs baseballs for the kids, dances. Ah old left bank carlos is throwing a party for genet's new anthology subjective laughter cures. Now carl in his pink maryland riding habit sings the new hit tune, going goer going for gone, Now carl begins to write ballads & think immortal & comb his hair into a peak that had snow on it, How sudden the memory of the beethoven quartets, the agonies, returned to man, totaled on a dark ear. & now chessman cites the bull, manolete glowers, chessman reminds him that he is dead, blacked out, old aficionado carlito warns manolo to stay away from dead movie stars, sudden death for dead . . . . bull fighters, chessman invents a new drug that cures kleptomania, & locates nuns arabia.

Now the pat o'brien leading man demands that stonewall chessman cop out, the idiot . . . . the worried football player tried to fumble, but old gentleman jim chessman is telephoning . . . . & now chessman predicts the arrival of the damp movie stars, not included in the tarot . . . . & with them is the brightest of these year round christmas trees, orphans of the camus storm, & the celebrated subliminal commercial blinking across their sincere suits, VICTIM WILLING & now doctor von stroheim is explaining how the two miniature atom bombs set each other off in that little gray pail that the guards are putting a coat of lipstick on right now . . . . . . & the committed slide along the bagel shop walls, satirical quentical of the mind.

Here, Chessman, is the message to all garcias everywhere, longitude people, beyond the margin,

I am glad now, sad now, home, in TIME FOR THE MURDER, guilty California is quiet

THE ENORMOUS GAS BILL AT THE DWARF FACTORY.
A HORROR MOVIE TO BE SHOT WITH EYES.

(Dedicated to the Mothers of America.)

(REEL I)

Carl Chessman interviews San Quentin P.T.A. before leaving on
his . . . . annual tour of California Death U-niversities.

Caryl Chess- Man is in sickly California writing death threats to
the Wizard of Oz, the green giant announces his trial will be held
in the stomach of . . . . Junipero Serra.

Charlie Chaplin & Sitting Bull walk hand in hand through the
World Series, Chest- Mann steals all the bases except Home &
receives the last sack-o-men from KING KONG.

Oyez, Oyez, Oyez, the people of the state of Call CHEZ- Main vs
CALIFORNIA. Caul enters the plaza dressed in blinking RED-
LIGHTS singing clap hands . . . . . here comes the lindberg baby, pre-
sents the Judge with an impressionistic . . . . . picture of Sebastian
with three beautiful stink flowers growing in his ear . . . declares
MOTHERS DAY out of bounds for spacemen, winks at the GOLD
STAR . . . . FATHERS, offers to sculpt their souls into exotic
shapes, without charge . . . .

End of reel one.

ALL BOOM SHOOTING TO BE DONE FROM FAR OUT . . . .
CLOSEUPS TO BE SHOT ZOOMING IN . . . CAMERA PANS THE SET
ON THE WAY BACK OUT . . . . . .

Film to be used in shooting reel one. BLACK OR WHITE OR COLOR, NOT YET DEVELOPED OR DEVELOPED ALREADY.

Props to be used on this location . . . . ONE RUSTY OFFIZCIAL BUCKET, ONE SAWED OFF HIGH CHAIR.

(REEL II)

As the scene opens wave after wave of twin-engined attorney generals fly past . . . . . . dipping their wings as tho' passing over the tomb of the unknown gas meter . . . .

Caryl Mellville writes first book on new butane concept of humility . . . . CELL No. Pennsylvania 6-5000, Waitun Place.
CARL DARROW APPEARS IN COURT WITHOUT SUSPENDERS OR MAKE-UP & a brilliant monkey . . . . perched on each eyelid, submits STARTLING legal brief on bailiff's unshined shoe . . . .
Prima Faeces Nolo Contendere Argument on old little known decision in . . . . obscure criminal case, "THE PEOPLE OF MARIN COUNTY VS. I. SOCRATES" . . . . forgotten trial hinged on whether or not the prosecutor was plugged into proper wall . . .
. . . . . socket while preparing case, ended in hung plaintiffs, daring move wins populautor new trial, judge sets new hearing for opening day of famous salinas rodeshowdown session to be held in castroville, "artichoke capital of the world" . . . .

(MONTAGE SEQUENCE):

OPENS ON DAVY CROCKETT IN COONSKIN KNICKERS STANDING IN FRONT OF A SHOOTING . . . . GALLERY ON FORTY SECOND STREET BUYING ONE HUNDRED ROUNDS FOR A QUARTER, CLOSE-UP OF A GRIM-FACED CONGRESSMAN SHOOTING AT LITTLE CAST IRON BEARS, CLUSTERS OF LITTLE UNCRACKED LIBERTY

BELLS DANGLE FROM HIS EARS, THREE UNLIT BIRTHDAY CAN-
DLES GROW SLOWLY FROM HIS HEAD AS THE LAST BEAR
KNEELS DOWN & EXPENSIVE RAIN FALLS, EMERGING FROM
THIS FRAME SUDDENLY WE SEE GAYLY DECORATED LANDING
CRAFT . . . . BULGING WITH FIERCE LOOKING PENGUINS
ALL WEARING SHINY NEW WRIST WATCHES & . . . . SMOK-
ING ROLL YOUR OWN CIGARETTES, THE SMOKE FORMING A
HUGE CLOUD THAT TURNS . . . . . INTO A GIGANTIC, LUSTY, RAW,
PAGAN, JIVARO TEENAGER PURSUED BY FOUR MIDWESTERN
ALBINOS THROWING PEPPERMINT JAVELINS AT HER REVOLVING
BREAST BEFORE BEING FELLED BY A NUCLEAR TIPPED SNOW-
BALL. THROWN BY NANOOK OF THE NORTH., SCENE ENDS WITH
NANOOK PASSING OUT SOUVENIR POLAR BEARS AT THE GRAND
OPENING OF THE NEW ARNOLD SHOENBERG SUPERMARKET,
WHILE OUTSIDE IT IS RAINING BLACK VOLKSWAGENS (*END OF
MONTAGE SEQUENCE*) FILM RETURNS TO ENORMOUS GAS BILL.

*(AT THIS POINT FILM SHOULD ANNOUNCE THAT IT IS VERY CROWDED AT
DISNEYLAND).*

It is now summer for the one Billionth consecutive time & once
more Caruso sings take me out to the ball game as Yankee Stadium
fills up with Zionist & . . . . hardware store owners, old south-
paw Caryl watches as jane darwell throws out the first telephone
booth, the air is filled with invisible home runs & the . . . . crowd
cheers as the bleachers go up hometown flames, & Gertrude Stein
arrives in her private underground railroad car, surrounded by
know something intellectual WITH STILL LIFES in their eyes, & no
navels, WATCHING LEARNEDLY AS OLD CARL RUTH, LAST OF . . . .
THE OLD GASHOUSE GANG GOES DEEP INTO LEFT FIELD, HIS
BACK TO THE WALL, ALL EYES GLUED TO HIS DIFFICULT BREATH-
ING, AS HE WALKS INTO THE GRANDSTAND & THE BALL FALLS,
OUTSIDE THE FOUL LINE, OUT OF PLAY, THE UMPIRES ORDER
LEFTY CHESSMAN OUT OF THE STADIUM, BACK TO HIS SWANKY

BACHELOR APT, IN THE EL MUERTO HOTEL. WE LEAVE F. SCOTT CHESSMAN SITTING IN HIS WRITING DEN ON GLAMOROUS DEATH ROW, HE IS LEANING INTENTLY OVER THE TOILET BOWL NEAR HIS TYPEWRITER IN WHICH HE IS SECRETLY TRAINING HIS PET GOLD FISH, BROWNIE, TO SWIM THE ENGLISH CHANNEL, & NOW & THEN LOOKING UP TO COUNT THE LIFELIKE BLACK WIDOW SPIDERS ON WALLPAPER DONATED BY THE SATURDAY EVENING POST, & SO AS QUAINT LI'L' OLE WESTERN CIVILIZATION . . . . . . SINKS SLOWLY IN THE WEST, WE LEAVE FUN-LOVING CALIFORNIA WITH ALL OF ITS . . . COLORFUL DEATH FESTIVALS, & SET SAIL FOR EXOTIC NEBRASKA, CAREFREE GOTHIC ISLE, BIRTHPLACE OF THE FAMOUS INDIAN BONE SCULPTORS, ORIGINATORS OF THE CUSTER OPEN AIR HEAD, PAT. PENDING

(REEL III)

The scene opens with Dim Pictures of Animal Sadness, the Deathbed of the last Buffalo in Nebraska, he is dying of lonesomeness, (strange Plague Brought by The Ghost People), Weeping Beneath His Holy White Hide, he recalls cherished Memories of his past, Remembering when Indians were Red, recalling the Arrows Arc, Flamer the Soft Bull of the Skies, assuming his Bison Dignity, He refuses to be pitied or accompanied, Finally alone he unlocks the Acres of Unscarred American Love . . . . hidden in the boney caves of his great Mountainous Shaggy Godhead, Across the Green Centuries of his Eyes, his Soul walks the slaughtered plain His sheen of unreleased Contempt illuminates the one hundred million hushed Crucifixions buried in the bloody weave of triumphant Blue, Indigenous Murder cloth, His spirit erupts in punctual Geysers, unseen by the Roman eyes of Cold . . . Ohio People spreading Picnics & circuses, smearing katsup on the holy Playground His ancient Dream pounds with life, long vanished into leather Jackets . . . . His Fuming Wounds Burn in

Indignation, kindled by jets of hateful greed. The winds of lamentations carry his grief to be impaled on the Grand Tetons Arrowhead crown His Iconed Hide decorated forever with the Christmas Bullets of America . . . . . Arkward his Clean Beast Speech calls to his teeth, now hanging from the . . . . venereal wrist of the latest celluloid Madonna, grinning behind her prize-winning scabs . . . . Childlike Breezes Singing on the Rug of Skull Breathe the old litany of . . . Buried America's retelling Tribal Woes of ingenuously executed thin-lipped Pogroms. On the Rim of Ice White Extinction The Dying Buffalo Becomes the Scorned . . . . Image of Christ, His Compassionate Pawing uncovers the Mass Graves long . . . . concealed by Cowboy Death Games, Played by Men, America's Deadly Children . . . .

Emptied at last Chains of Lifeless Nebraskas string beadlike over the Stolen Landscape, Flat in emulation of its spidery soul, The Gaunt Stretches of Arid Guilt tints the surface of America's Pride, Sick pasted Repairs define those Terrifying Craters dug from the Confiscated Souls of Destroyed Giants Stashed behind Christian . . . . Altars, to be dragged out on Trophy days in Honor of Ancestral Kills . . . . Grinning in Consumptive Triumph, Subdividing the Happy Hunting Ground . . . . Clothed in Unfitting Garments peeled from Red Bodies of Wild Peace-Pipe Saints, Martyred by their Undying faithfulness to the caressing Earth, & This America's own Secret Deaths . . . . The bitter Nebraskas are finally dipped in the Blood, & no Lambs Bless Them, Leafless Nebraska's Stolen pool feeds on Laughing Springs drilled out of the Papoose Eyes of Black Banged Familiar Infants, The Native Baptism Stains America's Ragged Soul With Black Water . . . . & Gothic Hate Festivals of Rotted Conscience, suffocate the Vanishing Ambition, CARYL CHESSMAN WAS AN AMERICAN BUFFALO, THUNDERING ACROSS CALIFORNIA'S LYING PRAIRIES, RACKED WITH POISON THE ARROWS OF AUTHORITY, GUARDING THE BRILLIANT . . . . VISIONS OF MILLIONS OF

GENOCIDED RED CRAZY HORSE PEOPLE, DEAD IN THE MAKESHIFT GAS CHAMBERS OF SUPPRESSED HISTORY, CARL CHESSMAN WAS AN AMERICAN BUFFALO FILLED WITH GLISTEN-ING EMBRYOS, FLYING WITH ZULU KINGS TO THE BOTTOMLESS PITS OF AMERICA'S SOUL, CARYL CHESSMAN WAS AN AMERICAN BUFFALO, & OUR VOMITTING ASSASSINS KILLED HIM, & DESTROYED THEMSELVES IN THEIR REPUBLICAN-DEMOCRAT HASTE TO EXTINGUISH HIS BURNING. COME BY SMALL BROWN SON, TASTE HIS BREATH, SHINING US WITH TRUTH

(REEL IV)

The Natural Gass Ballard & The Germ At its Source.

The scene opens with dim silhouettes of animal sadness, trapped in echo chambers of time. We are standing at the death bed of the last Buffalo in Nebraska. he is dying of onesomeness, strange dis-ease brought by the new mirror people with no sky in their faces, unseen red fingers clutch at his snowy white hide holy in the light of love willful destruction.

Saturated with the rusty terra cotta dignity of Bisons, he refuses pity, & embarks on his dusty voyage alone.

Comforted by the promised shadows of the Great Divide, he unlocks the final hoard of raw American love, whispering it on the winds, blessed with the scars of terror.

Battering with his monumental hooves he grinds the remains of his injected fear into the dust of multiplied generations, releasing the inhibited future.

Across the layers of centuries stacked in his eyes, his soul traverses the newly slaughtered brain, singing benedictions learned from holy birds.

He bathes in geysers pushed from yesterday to zombie congregations of cold Nebraska people, alarm clocks in their claws, timing the orgasm of earth.

His steaming eyes seek out familiar caves to receive his hide, having seen his race become leather jackets on pimply backs of Nebraska masturbators.

His wounds become inflammatory beacons, ignited by Nebraska's matchbooks.

Damp winds of tomorrow carry his grief to impalement on Grand Tetons Arrow.

His hide becomes the brown Christmas tree of remorse, lit by America's blinking Christmas bullets.

His golden beast tongue screams for his stolen teeth, now hanging from the venereal wrist of Hollywood's latest madonna, posing in her glamorous scabs.

The eternal chorale of the breeze sings the litany of the red Phoenix . . . . the falling waters chant of nations of woe, the horror song cycle . . . . desperate retellings of the thin-lipped Nebraska pogroms . . . .

ALIEN WINDS

Alien winds sweeping the highway
fling the dust of medicine men,
    long dead,
        in the california afternoon

Into the floating eyes
    of spitting gadget salesmen,
    eating murdered hot dogs,
        in the california afternoon.

The ancient hindu guru
dreams of alabama,
gingerbread visions,
    of angry policemen,
    as he waves a sacred raga,
    over the breast of
        frigid sunworshippers,
        in the california afternoon

A sad-eyed mexican,
sacrifices an easter-faced virgin,
    to a cynical god,
        beneath an ancient sun,
        in the california afternoon.

thin fluted riddles . . . .
    yogi blown through lost ages . . . .
        discreet puddles, seeping . . . .
           down the back, of giant time . . . .
           caught in ankle deep theories . . . .
           of wind blown love . . . .

All those
floodlight monumental
    conceptions, along the road, laughing in wounded
        air,
        crying to paint me blue, in the california
           afternoon.

TIDAL FRICTION

Tidal Friction . . . Comments At Real Movie . . . . Something
KNOWS PITY can THROW us ERECTERS, SEEING-EYE MEN FOR . .
. . . . . . BLIND DOGS . . . ENTERFECTUALS . . .

Tidal Power . . .

. . . Jack-Hammering the Mind Mine . . .
Digging the Hole in the Soul . . . . Turn
in your seals & number the dust I
want to ask a terrifying question What
time is it going to be . . . . . The Tragedy
is, an over abundance . . . . of color, & a
total lack of black . . . . & between the
screams, Rancid function & America
boying you to manless death, no, not
even the great American novel of dis-
play, You bought That Death on . . .
time, & your only legacy is surplus . . . &
your America is a tinted mother whose
breast you have never sucked for all your
mimed lust, & the literature of your sui-
cide note is the significant arithmetic of
the remaindered calendar that mark the
filling of your hole in this American
place, from which you have been gone a
truly long time, & walked here since,
the trousered whore of your face, that
hand-painted mirror, stained with your
neutral presence, & the holes you call
eyes, & as you go endlessly Pin-striped
to wherever it is that you go, remember

I have never refused you my own
humaness, tho' yours are but nerveless .
. . . bites, for which I am in your per-
verse debt, for you have allowed me to
taste my blood, red with my own hot
living & it cooled my soul & I leave
your own sawdust within, for who . . .
would bite the dead, not even a know-
nothing intellectual, happy enough to
point his laughing finger at millions
postered sams, in fake star suit, & shout
i want you, while dancing on exotic
beds, but watch it scout, I can see those
gothic brain surgeons weeping over the
remains of destroyed american love
machines, & those know something
intellectuals hang around together, &
swap commentaries.

A TERROR IS MORE CERTAIN . . .

A terror is more certain than all the rare desirable popular songs i know, than even now when all of my myths have become . . . , & walk around in black shiny galoshes & carry dirty laundry to & fro, & read great books & don't know criminals intimately, & publish fat books of the month & have wifeys that are lousy in bed & never realize how bad my writing is because i am poor & symbolize myself.

A certain desirable is more terror to me than all that's rare, How come they don't give an academic award to all the movie stars that die? they're still acting, ain't they? even if they are dead, it should not be held against them, after all they still have the public on their side, how would you like to be a dead movie star & have people sitting on your grave?

A rare me is more certain than desirable, that's all the terror, there are too many basketball players in this world & too much progress in the burial industry, lets have old fashioned funerals & stand around & forgive & borrow wet handkerchiefs, & sneak out for drinks & help load the guy into the wagon, & feel sad & make a date with the widow & believe we don't see all of the people sinking into the subways going to basketball games & designing baby sitters at Madison Square Garden.

A certain me is desirable, what is so rare as air in a Poem, why can't i write a foreign movie like all the other boys my age, I confess to all the crimes committed during the month of April, but not to save my own neck, which is adjustable, & telescopes into any size noose, I'm doing it to save Gertrude Stein's reputation, who is secretly flying model airplanes for the underground railroad stern gang of oz, & is the favorite in all the bouts . . . not officially opened yet Holland tunnel is the one who writes untrue phone numbers.

A desirable poem is more rare than rare, & terror is certain, who wants to be a poet & work a twenty four hour shift, they never ask you first, who wants to listen to the radiator play string quartets all night. I want to be allowed not to be, suppose a man wants to swing on the kiddie swings, should people be allowed to stab him with queer looks & drag him off to bed & its no fun on top of a lady when her hair is full of shiny little machines & your ass reflected in that television screen, who wants to be a poet if you fuck on t.v. & all those cowboys watching.

SHEILA

CAST
OUT OF RAINCLOUDS
IN DAMPENED WINGS
MADE
LEWD CAUSTIC REMARKS
TO
THIRSTY OLD MEN
RIDING
WHEEZING GREY HORSES
ON
WARPED FADED CAROUSELS

REFLECTED EYES OF SWANS EMPTY AT LAST . . .

SHE IS GONE IN CAVES OF GREY MARBLE AND FORMS
SHE IS GONE IN BLUE TRUCKS PAINTED WITH SECRETS
SHE IS GONE IN TAXABLE PUBLIC SHEETS
SHE IS GONE IN CADAVER-INFESTED MUNICIPAL FILING CABINETS
SHE IS GONE IN STILLED WHIRLPOOLS PITTED ALONG HER ARMS
SHE IS GONE IN OBSCURE CONSIDERATION OF LOST EVENTS
SHE IS GONE IN COLD METROPOLITAN STATISTICS
SHE IS GONE IN SILENCE TO SILENCE FROM SILENCE
SHE IS GONE IN SHOES, IN SOCKS IN FABRICS OF BLACK
SHE IS GONE DRAGGING UNNOTICED ASPECTS OF US ALL

MOUNT THE TROPHY, THE WINNERS ARE WAITING
IN LIVING
ROOMS

You know Heather Bell, she lives around the corner from every-
body, Heather's problem is not staying around the corner . . . she is
an unusual girl, she has no desire to sleep with her father, partially
because her father is dead. It may also be said of her that she has
never willingly submitted to her stepfather . . . until she had
received everything she had been promised.

Heather is cool for a schoolgirl, she prefers the company of hipsters,
beats, homosexuals—impotent novelists . . . and a beat girl who looks
very much like a view of her as seen from the inside . . . . Heather
loves jazz as much as she hates her mother who no longer
loves . . . Heather is an American matador. Heather's mother is an
American bull. Heather needs a cape to tire her bull and prepare it
for the kill . . . Heather fights rough, her cape is apt to be ripped,
but how important is a cape when you know the important thing is
to kill. Heather is cool & needs a cool cape.

WALKING HOT SEASONS

From walking hot seasons, through unmarked years of light,
My face is moonburned, EVERYTHING THAT NEVER HAPPENED IS MY
FAULT.

BLACK CARROT OF DENIAL, BURNED IN THE TOASTERS OF MEMORY
THAT SUMMER NEVER CAME AGAIN, WE LIE IN THIGHS, SPEAKING
IN TONGUES, HOLY
BENT TURTLE OF REMORSE LOCKED IN STEP, CHASING THE HARE OF
WHIMSY,
EUPHORIC FIXER, UNCALL MY NAME, TEAR UP MY EYES, I REFUSE TO
APPEAR
THOSE THINGS DONE IN COMPASSION & TOTAL DISREGARD.
THOSE THINGS DONE BY PEOPLE I DIDN'T KNOW & PEOPLE
WHO KNEW ME,
EVERYTHING I PLANNED CAME AS A COMPLETE SURPRISE
THERE WERE NO INTERMISSIONS SO I WALKED OUT BEFORE
THE END.
THEY SAY MY LIFE IS EXCITING, BUT I DON'T BELIEVE THEM.

RESULTS OF A LIE DETECTOR TEST

From the sleeping calendar I have stolen a month
I am afraid to look at it, I don't want to know its name
Clenched in my fist I can feel its frost, its icy face
I cannot face the bewildered summer with a pocketful of snow
I imagine the accusing fingers of children who will never be born
How to shut out the cries of suffering death wishers, awaiting
      the silent doors of winter tombs. Deprived of cherished exits,
I shall never again steal a month . . . or a week or a day or an hour
  or a minute or a second, unless I become desperate again.

COME

Come let us journey to
        the Sky,
I promised the Moon.

All that I come from
All that I have been,
All that I am
All that I come to
All that I touch,
Blossoms from
        a thorn,
AROSEAROSE

Love is the condition
of Human Beings
Being Human.

To be beloved
Is all I need
And whom I love
Is loved indeed,
There never was a Night that
Ended, or began,

Forms breaking
Structures imaged,
Come love,
Love come.

Note: This was written for Eileen and Bob's first marriage in Mexico in
1958, and was read at their remarriage on Mt. Tamalpais, on September 6,
1976.

SARASWATI

May Saraswati give thee
       intelligence
Entwined with the Lotus . .
     Thou art produced from
       Limb by limb.
But of the heart thou art
        born!
Thou indeed are the
     self called son!
So live a hundred autumns

UNHISTORICAL EVENTS

APOLLINAIRE
>   NEVER KNEW ABOUT ROCK GUT CHARLIE
>   WHO GAVE FIFTY CENTS TO A POLICEMAN
>   DRIVING AROUND IN A 1927 NASH

APOLLINAIRE
>   NEVER MET CINDER BOTTOM BLUE,
>   FAT SAXOPHONE PLAYER WHO LAUGHED
>   WHILE PLAYING AND HAD STEEL TEETH

APOLLINAIRE
>   NEVER HIKED IN PAPIER MACHE WOODS
>   AND HAD A SCOUTMASTER WHO WROTE A SONG ABOUT
>   IVORY SOAP AND HAD A BAPTIST FUNERAL

APOLLINAIRE
>   NEVER SAILED WITH RIFF RAFF ROLFE
>   WHO WAS RICH IN CALIFORNIA, BUT
>   HAD TO FLEE BECAUSE HE WAS QUEER

APOLLINAIRE
>   NEVER DRANK WITH LADY CHOPPY WINE,
>   PEERLESS FEMALE DRUNK, WHO TALKED TO SHRUBS
>   AND MADE CHILDREN SING IN THE STREETS

APOLLINAIRE
>   NEVER SLEPT ALL NIGHT IN AN ICEHOUSE,
>   WAITING FOR SEBASTIAN TO RISE FROM THE AMMONIA
>   TANKS
>   AND SHOW HIM THE LITTLE UNPAINTED ARROWS.

COCOA MORNING

Variations on a theme by morning,
Two lady birds move in the distance.
Gray jail looming, bathed in sunlight.
Violin tongues whispering.

Drummer, hummer on the floor,
dreaming of wild beats, softer still,
Yet free of violent city noise,
Please, sweet morning,
Stay here forever.

PICASSO'S BALCONY

Pale morning light, dying in shadows, loving the earth in midday rays, casting blue to skies in rings, sowing powder trails across balconies. Hung in evening to swing gently, on shoulders of time, growing old, yet swallowing events of a thousand nights of dying and loving, all blue. Gone to that tomb, hidden in cubic air, breathing sounds of sorrow.

Crying love rising from the lips of wounded flowers, wailing, sobbing, breathing uneven sounds of sorrow, lying in wells of earth, throbbing, covered with desperate laughter, out of cool angels, spread over night. Dancing blue images, shades of blue pasts, all yesterdays, tomorrows, breaking on pebbled bodies, on sands of blue and coral, spent.

Life lying heaped in mounds, with volcano mouth tops, puckered, open, sucking in atoms of air, sprinkling in atoms of air, coloring space, with flecks of brilliance, opaline glistening, in eyes, in flames.

Blue flames burning, on rusty cliffs, overlooking blue seas, bluish. In sad times, hurt seabirds come to wail in ice white wind, alone, and wail in starlight wells, cold pits of evening, and endings, flinging rounds of flame sheeted balls of jagged bone, eaten, with remains of torn flowers, overwhelming afterthoughts, blinding loves, classic pains, casting elongated shadows, of early blue.

Stringing hours together in thin melodic lines, wrapped around the pearl neck of morning, beneath the laughter, of sad sea birds.

"MICHAELANGELO" THE ELDER

I live alone, like pith in a tree,
My teeth rattle, like musical instruments.
In one ear a spider spins its web of eyes,
In the other a cricket chirps all night,
This is the end,
Which art, that proves my glory has brought me.
I would die for Poetry.

BLUE SLANTED INTO BLUENESS

NO SEBASTIAN, NOT AGAIN, NOR A FIRST TIME EITHER
WHO WILL BE THE FIRST ONE TO BREAK THE ICE,
REST FOREVER IN THE AMMONIA TANK, IN AN ICE HOUSE
HUNG BY THE THUMBS.

> I AM NOT A FORM,
> I AM ME, SACRED & HOLY,
> I AM UNIMPALABLE,
> THE FORM THAT MEMORY TAKES
> HAS BLED ON ME,
> AND BURNED RIMBAUD TO ASHES,
> NO ONE ELSE CAN EVEN THINK OF THAT FORM
> BLEEDING THEMSELVES OR OTHERS.

EARLY LOVES

Slippery driftwood, icebreaking mudpacks.
Garfish, mothers of cajun whores,
Laughing blood noises, at comic shrimps.
Gliding on leaves of sunken trees.

Dying love, hidden in misty Bayous
Red love, turning black, brown,
Dead in the belly, brittle womb
Of some laughing crab.

A father. Whose, mine?
Floating on seaweed rugs.
To that pearl tomb, shining
Beneath my bayou's floor.

Dead, and dead,
And you dead too.

No more arm twisting,
Heart twisting laughter.
Dead moss, colors of sorrow.

Later in hot arms, hers,
Between sweaty lovemakings.
Crying will wet moss swamps,
Hidden beneath her arms.

Tears will wash her dirty murdered soul.
God will be called to atone for his sins.

ROUND ABOUT MIDNIGHT

Jazz radio on a midnight kick,
Round about Midnight,

Sitting on the bed,
With a jazz type chick
Round about Midnight,

Piano laughter, in my ears,
Round about Midnight.

Stirring laughter, dying tears,
Round about Midnight.

Soft blue voices, muted grins,
Exciting voices, Father's sins,
Round about Midnight.

Come on baby, take off your clothes,
Round about Midnight.

JAZZ CHICK

Music from her breast vibrating
Soundseared into burnished velvet.
Silent hips deceiving fools.
Rivulets of trickling ecstasy
From the alabaster pools of Jazz
Where music cools hot souls.
Eyes more articulately silent
Than Medusa's thousand tongues.
A bridge of eyes, consenting smiles
Reveal her presence singing
Of cool remembrance, happy balls
Wrapped in swinging
Jazz
Her music . . .
Jazz.

TEQUILA JAZZ

The party is on.
People are on,
Too.
Are you on too?

Who crouches there in my
Heart?
Some wounded bird,
Hidden in the tall grass
That surrounds my heart.

Unseen wings of jazz,
Flapping, flapping.
Carry me off, carry me off.
Dirt of a world covers me,
My secret heart,
Beating with unheard jazz.

Thin melody ropes
Entwine my neck,
Hanging with
Tequila smiles,
Hanging, Man,
Hanging.

HARWOOD ALLEY SONG (San Francisco)

Oh the God-bus has a busted wheel
Oh Atlantis died of venereal disease
Caesar's hung on Pandora's box
Mexico Mexico, fill my nostrils.

Rimbaud, you brilliant maniac, desert turtle.
Stop flirting with camels, turn in your pike,
we are late for the lotus affair, sacrifice,
after Bacchanal, the form shall bleed, on us.

Remnants of neo-classical witch doctors,
hurling jagged missives of flame-sheeted bone,
affecting space cures, on curved people,
standing in themselves, up to their necks.

Inside my cave-eyes the desperate cock
fled shrieking, deserting my handless clock.
God, you are just an empty refrigerator;
with a dead child inside, incognito,
in the debris of the modern junkpile.

Nut-brown hands, hot from pushing Paracutin
from smoky core, to exploding light, reddened,
must yet calm vibrant nerves of dead gods,
yet tear Montezuma, from dark skies,
to chant the song of time, for us.

Warm-blooded petitions, demanding unnoticed existence,
voided by sudden accusations, abstract dares,
trapped in moist webs of atoms, secreted,
in folds of wind, caught hanging in time.

Note: Harwood Alley was renamed Bob Kaufman Street by the city of San
Francisco, October 2, 1988.

HIS HORN

Swinging horn softly confirming
Anguished cries of eternal losers
Whose gifts outgrow their presence.
We hear this lonesome Saxworld dweller
Swing higher—
Defiantly into a challenge key
Screamed over a heartbeat
Shouting at all beat seekers
To vanish into soft sounds of jazz
And walk with him to smoky ends
While his jazz walks forever
Across our parched heartstrings.

THE BIGGEST FISHERMAN

singular prints filed along damp banks,
supposed evidence of fouled strings, all,

breached dikes of teeth hewn agate statues
scaly echoes in eroded huts of slate and gristle.

mildewed toes of pastoral escapes, mossy charades,
cane towered blind, smooth blister on watern neck

angry glowing fish in eniwetok garments and pig tusks
alarmed horror of black croakers, finned hawks sinking.

collectors of fish teeth and souls of night vision demons
taxidermy fiesta of revolutionary aquatic holidays lost.

breeding hills of happy men, of no particular bent, or none,
condemned to undreamlike beauty of day to day to day to day,
deprived of night, ribbon bright streams die parched deaths
baked by fissioning waves of newly glowing fish.

INSIDE CONNIE

INNER LIT, TWISTED TREES,

SNARLING.

CURTAINS OF THE MIND,

DRAWN.

EXPOSING MADNESS,

ILLUMINATING DEATH,

DANCING,

AROUND HER HEAD.

LOST WINDOW

Tall strips of carrion moonlight.
Sparing only stars.
Giant bees gliding along the sidewalks,
Lonely insects, stinging each other.
Unknowing victims, mounting feathery scaffolds.
Lines of tired aprons dancing mobile-like
Across lit stages of air.
Minute pieces of death, flinging themselves
Across crowded intersections.
Muted sobbing of a hidden child,
Filters over the sill
Of a secret window, hidden
In the dark corner
Of evening.

CROSS WINDS (Song for Paul Swanson)

Cross wind, eat lost mad ones,
Cactus, grow them over.
Dig small graves, shallow.
Lay them gently
In the soft earth.
Speak the dead words,
Tell of life, lost.
Give places to the wanderers,
Corners, where they might crawl.
In the end, in beginnings,
Give love, give life,
At last, give death,
Cross winds.

BELIEVE, BELIEVE

Believe in this. Young apple seeds,
In blue skies, radiating young breast,
Not in blue-suited insects,
Infesting society's garments.

Believe in the swinging sounds of jazz,
Tearing the night into intricate shreds,
Putting it back together again,
In cool logical patterns,
Not in the sick controllers,
Who created only the Bomb.

Let the voices of dead poets
Ring louder in your ears
Than the screechings mouthed
In mildewed editorials.
Listen to the music of centuries,
Rising above the mushroom time.

BLUE O'CLOCK

Seven Floating lead moons,
    Red up night skies,
    Seven twisted horns,
    Mouth blown seven times.
Seven shaking angels
    Shadowed stripe,
    Night.
    Seven ice white suns,
    White down day skies,
    Revealing our pains
    To each.

[BUT AS LOVE]

BUT AS LOVE

IS

LONG-WINDED

THE MOVING WIND

DESCRIBED ITS

MOVING COLORS

IN SOUND &

LIGHT.

THE CAT IS SLEEPING ON A POEM

A Lady cigarette fixed in the ash trays of history
I shall unremember last night's humorous junk tragedies
In honor of personal survival I turn my back to the mirror
The sun is an oatmeal cookie, the moon a blue glass eye
Hooked on fake wisdom, the owl's wing hides his eye in the light.

Sometimes a sacred dream is wrapped in scarf,
Thrown around an anonymous neck, & chest,
As smoking worlds emerge, hot flickering signals
From Indian nerves, in bonfires of Aztec surprises.

There is a season in the mind when
The toadstools change color.
Not hot, not cold,
It comes at no known
Times
Perhaps that china plate was
Exaggerating, maybe
The gingham dog, & the calico cat
Got married,
And lived happily ever after.

SUN

Sun, Creator of Suns,
Sun, which makes Men,
My eye fails me,
Longing to see Thee
I touch stone.
For the sole desire to know
Thee
Might I know thee
Might I consider thee
Might I understand
Look down upon me
Sun, Moon, Day, Night,
Spring, Winter,
Are not ordained in vain.

THE MIND FOR ALL ITS REASONING

The mind for all its complicated reasoning,
Is dependent on the whim of an eyelid,
The most nonchalant of human parts,
Opening and closing at random,
Spending its hours in mystique,
Filled with memories of glimpses
       & blinks.

An eyelid hurled at the moon,
An exhausted nude woman,
Damp kimonas flowing from her pores.

A red poem can be a
    Hairy fire-extinguisher
    Hanging from the ears of
    A divine burglar,
My eyes opened on closed windows, a curved man.

CROOTEY SONGO

DERRAT SLEGELATIONS, FLO GOOF BABER,
SCRASH SHO DUBIES, WAGO WAILO WAILO.
GEED BOP NAVA GLIED, NAVA GLIED NAVA,
SPLEERIEDER, HUYEDIST, HEDACAZ, AX——, O, O.

DEEREDITION, BOOMEDITION, SQUOM, SQUOM, SQUOM.
DEE BEETSTRAWIST, WAPAGO, LOCOEST, LOCORO, LO.
VOOMETEYEREEPETIOP, BOP, BOP, BOP, WHIPOLAT.

DEGET, SKLOKO, KURRITIF, PLOG, MANGI, PLOG MANGI,
CLOPO JAGO BREE, BREE, ASLOOPERED, AKINGO LABY.
ENGPOP, ENGPOP, BOP, PLOLO, PLOLO, BOP, BOP.

SLIGHT ALTERATIONS

I climb a red thread
To an unseen existence,
Broken free, somewhere,
Beyond the belts.

Ticks have abandoned
My astonished time.
The air littered
With demolished hours.

Presence abolished
I become a ray
From the sun
Anonymous finger
Deflected into hungry windows
Boomerang of curved light
Ricocheted off dark walls
The ceiling remembers my face
The floor is a palate of surprise
Watching me eat the calendar.

I SIGH A MARBLED SIGH AH, AT LAST.

WE FLY AHEAD INTO THE PAST, GOOD, WE DEFEAT PROGRESS,
PROGRESS HAS BECOME BALD GALL & STOLE GOLD GROWN
BENEATH A FALL OFF OF THESE WALLS OF NOW
      SO NEW, A DISAPPEARED YEBREAISHE, SO LONG AS WE
      SHOW A PROPHET.
         ANY LOSS WE GAIN IS HOURS, WHICH MULTIPLY AND
DIVIDE US INTO THE SEASONS OF APRIL, MONTH IN WHICH
MONTHS WERE BORN, & GO IF THEY REMEMBER NOT TO
REMEMBER ALL THOSE MEMORIES UNMARKED IN SEEDS &
ARROWS.

I HAVE MET THE ARTIST OF THE MOUNTING OF BLOCKS THAT
THIN THEMSELVES OUT INTO AN EYELINE DANCING COLOR
MOBILES STRETCHED FROM ONE EYE OF THE MIND TO ANOTH-
ER, & GOD FORBID, SHE IS NOT FORBIDDING, & THAT OMNIPO-
TENCE I FEARED WAS A PAINTING'S REVENGE FOR ALL THE
STARING IT HAS ENDURED AT THE HAND OF MY EYE, (TOUCHE,
ME COLOURS & STRUCTURES & ARTKEY TEXTURES WE ALL
WIND)

Why Write ABOUT

WRITE HUNG THINGS, MAD MESS
ZEN TREE JOY, DAD, LIKE, YOU KNOW?
SWUNG OUT CATS, HUNG,
ON PUBLICITY, LIKE, YOU KNOW.
SICK MIDDLE CLASS CHICKS,
NYMPHO, CACAUSOIDS, EATING SYMBOLS,
LITTLE OLD BOYS, IN MONDAY BEARDS,
ATTENDING, ALL THE, SCHOOLS,
OF SELF PITY,
SELLING THEIR RIGHT
TO REVOLUTION,
TO A PIECE OF,
LIKE, YOU KNOW MAN,
ITS, A SCENE,
LIKE, YOU KNOW,
THE, MOTHER BIT.

GENETIC COMPLICATIONS.
LIKE MAN, LIKE
MAN, LIKE,
LIKE.

WAITING

SOMEWHERE THERE WAITS, WAITING
A BOOK IS WAITING, WAITING,
TO BE WRITTEN.
COLD COLD PAGES, WAITING,
TO BE WRITTEN,
MAN SEEKS GOD,
IN A BOOK.

SOMEWHERE THERE WAITS, WAITING
A PICTURE WAITS, WAITING,
WAITING TO BE PAINTED
COLD COLD CANVAS, CANVAS.
WAITING TO BE PAINTED.
MAN SEEKS GOD IN A PICTURE.

SOMEWHERE THERE WAITS, WAITING
A WOMAN WAITING, WAITING,
TO BE LOVED, WAITING,
COLD COLD WOMAN,
WAITING TO BE LOVED,
MAN SEEKS GOD IN A WOMAN.

SOMEWHERE THERE WAITS, WAITING
A MAN IS WAITING, WAITING,
COLD COLD MAN, WAITING,
TO BE WANTED, WAITING.
MAN SEEKS GOD
IN MAN

SOMEWHERE THERE WAITS, WAITING
A BABY IS WAITING, WAITING.
WAITING, WAITING TO BE BORN,
COLD COLD BABY, WAITING,
TO BE BORN, BLOOD OF EARTH,
WAITING TO BE.
MAN SEEKS GOD,
IN A BABY.

WIND, SEA,
SKY, STARS,
SURROUND
US.

HEAVY WATER BLUES.

The radio is teaching my goldfish Jujutsu
I am in love with a skindiver who sleeps underwater,
My neighbors are drunken linguists, & I speak butterfly,
Consolidated Edison is threatening to cut off my brain,
The postman keeps putting sex in my mailbox,
My mirror died, & can't tell if i still reflect,
I put my eyes on a diet, my tears are gaining too much weight.

I crossed the desert in a taxicab
only to be locked in a pyramid
With the face of a dog
on my breath

I went to a masquerade
Disguised as myself
Not one of my friends
Recognized

I dreamed I went to John Mitchell's poetry party
in my maidenform brain

Put the silver in the barbeque pit
The Chinese are attacking with nuclear
Restaurants

The radio is teaching my goldfish Ju Jutsu
My old lady has taken up skin diving & sleeps underwater
I am hanging out with a drunken linguist, who can speak butterfly
And represents the caterpillar industry down in Washington D. C.

*

I never understand other peoples' desires or hopes,
until they coincide with my own, then we clash.

I have definite proof that the culture of the caveman,
disappeared due to his inability to produce one magazine,
that could be delivered by a kid on a bicycle.

When reading all those thick books on the life of god,
it should be noted that they were all written by men.

It is perfectly all right to cast the first stone,
if you have some more in your pocket.

Television, america's ultimate relief, from the indian disturbance.

I hope that when machines finally take over,
they won't build men that break down,
as soon as they're paid for.

i shall refuse to go to the moon,
unless i'm inoculated, against
the dangers of indiscriminate love.

After riding across the desert in a taxicab,
he discovered himself locked in a pyramid
with the face of a dog on his breath.

The search for the end of the circle,
constant occupation of squares.

Why don't they stop throwing symbols,
the air is cluttered enough with echoes.

Just when i cleaned the manger for the wisemen,
the shrews from across the street showed up.

The voice of the radio shouted, get up
do something to someone, but me & my son
laughed in our furnished room.

WHEN WE HEAR THE EYE OPEN . . .

When we hear the eye open, there, in that place,
There, a whisper is a scream,
Breathing there, in that place,
A breath is the birth of sound,
We shall see our reflections
On the gigantic thighs of a giant,
There, in that place,
My head is a bony guitar, strung with tongues, plucked by fingers &
    nails,
The giant is only his legs, the rest of him will be gone far on,
And blinking cities will fly from his knees,
    And in a future, in that place, there,
        I was a nut in a chocolate bar,
           And I melted in a soft hand,
             And we sang a luna tune,

The ear hears fear, the eye lies, the mind dies, the teeth curl,
And Runic stone alone, weeps at the death of sleep.
Colder than a frozen nun, chilly accusations point,
Naked river, screamer on lonely poet corners,
Yes, and bugs with lights another crime of mine
How else walk against these black winds of mind death,

Blowing down these lonely streets,
They have found a way to disturb the moon,
The sun burns at love's two ends,
On the eternal launching pad.

FALLING

Cool shadows blanked dead cities, falling,
Electric anthills, where love was murdered.
Daily crucifixions, on stainless steel crosses,
In the gardens of pillbox subdivisions, falling.
Poets, like free reeds, drift over fetid landscapes,
Bearded Phoenix, burning themselves, falling.
Death patterns capture the eyes, falling.
A saving madness, cast by leafless trees, falling,
Cushions the songs, filtered through smoking ruins,
From the nostrils of unburied dead gods.
Cool shadows, fall over drawn eyelids, falling,
Cutting off the edge of time, falling, endlessly.

I WISH . . .

I wish that whoever it is inside of me,
would stop all that moving around,
& go to sleep, another sleepless year
like the last one will drive me sane,

I refuse to have any more retired burglars
picking the locks on my skull, crawling in
through my open windows, i'll stay out forever,
or at least until spring, when all the wintered
minds turn green again,

It's all right fellows, it's just a joke,
you had me scared for a moment God, i thought you were serious,
i was beginning to believe that this was really your idea of life,
I know second fifth, but you made it sound so unbelievable,
You're the only one in this whole big universal gin mill, believe me
        god,
who could get away with it, even that oldest boy of yours
& yet even he, your own
fleshlessness & bloodlessness, was helpless when it came to dirty
        jokes.

SUICIDE

Big Fanny & stromin vinne deal,
all that's left of the largest colony
of the new world, who coulda guessed it
no one in his right mind.

Poets don't sneak into zoos & talk with tigers anymore,
even though they read Blake & startle all by striped
devices, while those poems of God pout, lurking & sundried torn tree
        jungles
William Blake never saw a tiger & never fucked a lamb.
you get off at fifty ninth street, forever

The first man was an idealist, but he died,
he couldn't survive the first truth,
discovering that the whole
world, all of it, was all his, he sat down
& with a little piece of string, & a sharp stone
invented suicide.

THE LATE LAMENTED WIND,
BURNED IN INDIGNATION

TONTO IS DEAD, TONTO IS DEAD, TONTO IS DEAD
      RUN HIDE IN SUBWAYS.
      ELECTRIC ARROW OF PENITENT MACHINES & FOOT-
STEP
      HORROR
    LET THE FLEA CIRCUS PERFORM, TONTO IS DEAD—

THE BEST PLACE TO JUDGE A TAP DANCE CONTEST,
      IS FROM BENEATH THE STAGE.
      TONTO IS DEAD, HIDE IN SUBWAYS.
HEAVY WATER MUSIC, SPILLED FROM PUBLIC HARPSICHORDS,

AT GALA LAUNDERMAT CONCERTS, FEATURING SONATAS FOR
DE-
      FEATED OBOES,
      BETWEEN DOOR SLAM OVERTURES, & SOGGY BALLETS,
      EXITING INTO KEY EYES OF LONELY JAZZERS,
        TONTO IS DEAD, TONTO IS DEAD,
          MUSEUMS ARE EXEMPT FROM MARTIAL LAW,
            HIDE IN THE SUBWAY, QUICK
            BEFORE IT MELTS.

NIGHT SUNG SAILOR'S PRAYER

Voyager now, on a ship of night
Off to a million midnights, black, black
Into forever tomorrows, black
Voyager off to the time worlds,
Of life times ending, bending, night.

Pleader on the ship of the children night
Begging a song for children still in flight
Sing little children, sing in the empty cathedrals
Sing in the vacant theaters,
Sing laughter to the twisted sons
Poisoned from the mildewed fathers
Sing love to the used up whores
Dying in some forgotten corner.
Sing sunlight and barking dogs
To the born losers, decaying in the sorry jails.

Sing pity and hell, to the wax bitches
Buried in the bowels of the male cadillacs
Sing tomorrow and tomorrow and sing maybe next time
To the negro millionaires, trapped in their luxurious complexions.

Sing love and an everlasting fix
For the hopeless junkies, stealing into night's long time
Sing yes, and yes, and more and more
To the cloud borne bohemians
Afloat in their endless fantasies.

Sing love and life and life and love
All that lives is Holy,
The unholiest, most holy all.

THE UNDER WEIGHT CHAMPION

What goes up is bound to come down . . .
What goes down is bound to come up.
For god's sake, stop all the stop
God is missing & is out trying to launch his own rocket.
Hooray for mrs. Rasputin.
Burnt eskimos to the rear march.
Adam & Eve went up the hill to fly a drunken garter,
Mrs. Jack horner sat in a corner eating her son's last pie,
Jack & Jill are guilty of eating stolen apples,
A kleptomaniac steals from bees, & has a many-armed mind,
Little miss muffet sat on a tuffet waiting for a taxi-cab.
Shear the hot cakes clean, the locust people are painting my
head, one beard explodes succession burned comedies
inside a head.

PLEA

Voyager, wanderer of the heart,
Off to
        a million midnights, black, black
Voyager, wanderer of star worlds,
Off to
        a million tomorrows, black, black,
Seek and find Hiroshima's children,
        Send them back, send them back.
Tear open concrete sealed cathedrals, spiritually locked
        Fill vacant theaters with their musty diversions,
Almost forgotten laughter.

Give us back the twisted sons
Poisoned by mildewed fathers.
Find again the used up whores,
Dying in some forgotten corner,
Find sunlight, and barking dogs,
For the lost, decayed in sorry jails.
Find pity, find Hell for wax bitches,
Hidden in the bowels of male Cadillacs.
Find tomorrow and next time for Negro millionaires
Hopelessly trapped in their luxurious complexions.
Find love, and an everlasting fix for hopeless junkies,
Stealing into lost nights, long time.

Voyager now,
        Off to a million midnights, black, black
Seek and find Hiroshima's children,
        Send them back, send them back.

DRUNK TIME

Free reeds drift in the weeping morning,
Here on the liquid floor of hell.
Phoenix, burn sunlight, to dead gods,
As concrete patterns capture eyes.

Poet madness aglow in the shadows,
Breathing songs amid the smoke
From the eyes of long dead gods,
Tall weeds walk on air,
Between your breath & mine.

Naked flint-eyed women,
Goddesses of nothing,
Brightly lit flesh,
Eaten, in rooms of the dead.

Cool shadows fall on drawn eyelids,
Drunken memories, weave in, out of times past,
Times of pear-shaped arguments,
Of intent & purpose,
Lost among crashing noises,
Cynical laughter,
Echoes of tears,
As the air ends

GENEOLOGY

Great-Grandfathers, blessed by great-grandmothers,
Shaped recently cooled buried stars, downed moons.

Creating hawk-beaked hatchets, phallic pikes, fire,
To tear out stubborn determined cells, clinging to
Other great-grandfathers, other great-grandmothers.

Proudly survived fathers, goaded by proud mothers,
Rolled lead drippings into skull piercing eternities.

Sent to stamp death on final presences, life forms,
Of other survived fathers, other proud mothers.

Sons, grandsons, daughters, granddaughters, bastards
Rolling the atmosphere into sinister nuclear spheres.

Insane combustions, to melt the bones, ivory teeth,
Of other sons, grandsons, daughters, granddaughters,
Bastards.

Here, Adam, take back your God damn rib.

ON

On yardbird corners of embryonic hopes, drowned in a heroin tear.
On yardbird corners of parker flights to sound filled pockets in space.
On neuro-corners of stripped brains & desperate electro-surgeons.
On alcohol corners of pointless discussions & historical hangovers.
On television corners of literary corn flakes & rockwells impotent
     America.
On university corners of tailored intellect & greek letter openers.
On military corners of megathon deaths & universal anesthesia.
On religious corners of theological limericks and
On radio corners of century-long records & static events.
On advertising corners of filter-tipped ice-cream & instant instants.
On teen-age corners of comic book seduction & corrupted guitars.
On political corners of wanted candidates & ritual lies.
On motion picture corners of lassie & other symbols.
On intellectual corners of conversational therapy & analyzed fear.
On newspaper corners of sexy headlines & scholarly comics.
On love divided corners of die now pay later mortuaries.
On philosophical corners of semantic desperadoes & idea-mongers.
On middle class corners of private school puberty & anatomical revolts.
On ultra-real corners of love on abandoned roller-coasters.
On lonely poet corners of low lying leaves & moist prophet eyes.

O-JAZZ-O

Where the string
At
Some point,
Was some umbilical jazz,
Or perhaps,
In memory,
A long lost bloody cross,
Buried in some steel calvary.
In what time
For whom do we bleed,
Lost notes, from some jazzman's
Broken needle.
Musical tears from lost
Eyes.
Broken drumsticks, why?
Pitter patter, boom dropping
Bombs in the middle
Of my emotions
My father's sound
My mother's sound,
Is love,
Is life.

O-JAZZ-O War Memoir: Jazz, Don't Listen To It At Your Own Risk

In the beginning, in the wet
Warm dark place,
Straining to break out, clawing at strange cables
Hearing her screams, laughing
"Later we forgave ourselves, we didn't know"
Some secret jazz
Shouted, *wait, don't go.*
Impatient, we came running, innocent
Laughing blobs of blood & faith.
To this mother, father world
Where laughter seems out of place
So we learned to cry, pleased
They pronounce human.
The secret Jazz blew a sigh
Some familiar sound shouted *wait*
Some are evil, some will hate.
"Just Jazz, blowing its top again"
So we rushed & laughed.
As we pushed & grabbed
While jazz blew in the night
Suddenly they were too busy to hear a simple sound
They were busy shoving mud in men's mouths,
Who were busy dying on the living ground
Busy earning medals, for killing children on deserted street corners
Occupying their fathers, raping their mothers, busy humans we
Busy burning Japanese in atomicolorcinemascope
With stereophonic screams,
What one hundred per cent red blooded savage, would waste precious
    time
Listening to jazz, with so many important things going on
But even the fittest murderers must rest

So they sat down in our blood soaked garments,
and listened to jazz
        lost, steeped in all our death dreams
They were shocked at the sound of life, long gone from our own
They were indignant at the whistling, thinking, singing, beating,
        swinging,
They wept for it, hugged, kissed it, loved it, joined it, we drank it,
Smoked it, ate with it, slept with it
They made our girls wear it for lovemaking
Instead of silly lace gowns,
Now in those terrible moments, when the dark memories come
The secret moments to which we admit no one
When guiltily we crawl back in time, reaching away from ourselves
They hear a familiar sound,
Jazz, scratching, digging, blueing, swinging jazz,
And listen,
And feel, & die.

Oct. 5th, 1963

Chronicle
Letters to the Editor
5th & Mission
San Francisco, Calif.

Gentlemen:

Arriving back in San Francisco to be greeted by a blacklist and eviction, I am writing these lines to the responsible non-people. One thing is certain I am not white. Thank God for that. It makes everything else bearable.

The Loneliness of the Long Distance Runner is due to the oneliness of the Long Distance Runner, that uniqueness that is the Long Distance Runner's alone, and only his. The Loneliness of the Long Distance Runner is the only reason for the Long Distance Runner's existence. Short distance runners run, they finish neither first nor last, they finish, that is all that can be said about them, nothing can be said for them, an ordinariness that is their closest proximity to the truly unique. Men die, as all men come to know, sooner or later, at any rate either way, men die. On that all men can depend.

To answer that rarely asked question . . . . Why are all blacklists white? Perhaps because all light lists are black, the listing of all that is listed is done by who is brown, the colors of an earthquake are black, brown & beige, on the Ellington scale, such sweet thunder, there is a silent beat in between the drums.

That silent beat makes the drumbeat, it makes the drum, it makes the beat. Without it there is no drum, no beat. It is not the beat played by who is beating the drum. His is a noisy loud one, the silent beat is beaten by who is not beating on the drum, his silent beat drowns out all the noise, it comes before and after every beat, you hear it in between, its sound is

Bob Kaufman, Poet

SOLITUDES CROWDED WITH LONELINESS

AFRICAN DREAM

In black core of night, it explodes
Silver thunder, rolling back my brain,
Bursting copper screens, memory worlds
Deep in star-fed beds of time,
Seducing my soul to diamond fires of night.
Faint outline, a ship—momentary fright
Lifted on waves of color,
Sunk in pits of light,
Drummed back through time,
Hummed back through mind,
Drumming, cracking the night.
Strange forest songs, skin sounds
Crashing through—no longer strange.
Incestuous yellow flowers tearing
Magic from the earth.
Moon-dipped rituals, led
By a scarlet god,
Caressed by ebony maidens
With daylight eyes,
Purple garments,
Noses that twitch,
Singing young girl songs
Of an ancient love
In dark, sunless places
Where memories are sealed,
Burned in eyes of tigers.

Suddenly wise, I fight the dream:
Green screams enfold my night.

WALKING PARKER HOME

Sweet beats of jazz impaled on slivers of wind
Kansas Black Morning/ First Horn Eyes/
Historical sound pictures on New Bird wings
People shouts/ boy alto dreams/ Tomorrow's
Gold belled pipe of stops and future Blues Times
Lurking Hawkins/ shadows of Lester/ realization
Bronze fingers—brain extensions seeking trapped sounds
Ghetto thoughts/ bandstand courage/ solo flight
Nerve-wracked suspicions of newer songs and doubts
New York altar city/ black tears/ secret disciples
Hammer horn pounding soul marks on unswinging gates
Culture gods/ mob sounds/ visions of spikes
Panic excursions to tribal Jazz wombs and transfusions
Heroin nights of birth/ and soaring/ over boppy new ground.
Smothered rage covering pyramids of notes spontaneously
        exploding
Cool revelations/ shrill hopes/ beauty speared into
        greedy ears
Birdland nights on bop mountains, windy saxophone
        revolutions.
Dayrooms of junk/ and melting walls and circling vultures/
Money cancer/ remembered pain/ terror flights/
Death and indestructible existence

In that Jazz corner of life
Wrapped in a mist of sound
His legacy, our Jazz-tinted dawn
Wailing his triumphs of oddly begotten dreams
Inviting the nerveless to feel once more
That fierce dying of humans consumed
In raging fires of Love.

AFTERWARDS, THEY SHALL DANCE

In the city of St. Francis they have taken down the statue of
　　St. Francis,
And the hummingbirds all fly forward to protest, humming
　　feather poems.

Bodenheim denounced everyone and wrote. Bodenheim had
　　no sweet marijuana dreams,
Patriotic muscateleer, did not die seriously, no poet love to
　　end with, gone.

Dylan took the stone cat's nap at St. Vincent's, vaticaned
　　beer, no defense;
That poem shouted from his nun-filled room, an insult to the
　　brain, nerves,
Save now from Swansea, white horses, beer birds, snore
　　poems, Wales-bird.

Billie Holiday got lost on the subway and stayed there
　　forever,
Raised little peace-of-mind gardens in out of the way
　　stations,
And will go on living in wrappers of jazz silence forever,
　　loved.

My face feels like a living emotional relief map, forever wet.
My hair is curling in anticipation of my own wild gardening.

Poor Edgar Allan Poe died translated, in unpressed pants,
　　ended in light,
Surrounded by ecstatic gold bugs, his hegira blessed
　　by Baudelaire's orgy.

Whether I am a poet or not, I use fifty dollars worth
     of air every day, cool.
In order to exist I hide behind stacks of red and blue poems
And open little sensuous parasols, singing the nail-in-
     the-foot song, drinking cool beatitudes.

BENEDICTION

Pale brown Moses went down to Egypt land
To let somebody's people go.
Keep him out of Florida, no UN there:
The poor governor is all alone,
With six hundred thousand illiterates.

America, I forgive you . . . I forgive you
Nailing black Jesus to an imported cross
Every six weeks in Dawson, Georgia.
America, I forgive you . . . I forgive you
Eating black children, I know your hunger.
America, I forgive you . . . I forgive you
Burning Japanese babies defensively—
I realize how necessary it was.
Your ancestor had beautiful thoughts in his brain.
His descendants are experts in real estate.
Your generals have mushrooming visions.
Every day your people get more and more
Cars, televisions, sickness, death dreams.
You must have been great
Alive.

GRANDFATHER WAS QUEER, TOO

He was first seen in a Louisiana bayou,
Playing chess with an intellectual lobster.
They burned his linoleum house alive
And sent that intellectual off to jail.
He wrote home very day, to no avail.
Grandfather had cut out, he couldn't raise the bail.

Next seen, skiing on some dusty Texas road,
An intellectual's soul hung from his ears,
Discussing politics with an unemployed butterfly.
They hung that poor butterfly, poor butterfly.
Grandfather had cut out, he couldn't raise the bail.

Next seen on the Arizona desert, walking,
Applying soothing poultices to the teeth
Of an aching mountain.
Dentists all over the state brought gauze balls,
Bandaged the mountain, buried it at sea.
Grandfather had cut out, he couldn't raise the bail.

Next seen in California, the top part,
Arranging a marriage, mating trees,
Crossing a rich redwood and a black pine.
He was exposed by the Boy Scouts of America.
The trees were arrested on a vag charge.
Grandfather cut out, he couldn't raise the bail.

Now I have seen him here. He is beat.
His girlfriend has green ears;
She is twenty-three months pregnant.
I kissed them both:
Live happily ever after.

BAGEL SHOP JAZZ

Shadow people, projected on coffee-shop walls.
Memory formed echoes of a generation past
Beating into now.

Nightfall creatures, eating each other
Over a noisy cup of coffee.

Mulberry-eyed girls in black stockings,
Smelling vaguely of mint jelly and last night's bongo
       drummer,
Making profound remarks on the shapes of navels,
Wondering how the short Sunset week
Became the long Grant Avenue night,
Love tinted, beat angels,
Doomed to see their coffee dreams
Crushed on the floors of time,
As they fling their arrow legs
To the heavens,
Losing their doubts in the beat.

Turtle-neck angel guys, black-haired dungaree guys,
Caesar-jawed, with synagogue eyes,
World travelers on the forty-one bus,
Mixing jazz with paint talk,
High rent, Bartok, classical murders,
The pot shortage and last night's bust.
Lost in a dream world,
Where time is told with a beat.

Coffee-faced Ivy Leaguers, in Cambridge jackets,
Whose personal Harvard was a Fillmore district step,
Weighted down with conga drums,

The ancestral cross, the Othello-laid curse,
Talking of Bird and Diz and Miles,
The secret terrible hurts,
Wrapped in cool hipster smiles,
Telling themselves, under the talk,
This shot must be the end,
Hoping the beat is really the truth.

The guilty police arrive.

Brief, beautiful shadows, burned on walls of night.

REFLECTIONS ON A SMALL PARADE

When I see the little Buddhist scouts
Marching with their Zen mothers
To tea ceremonies at the rock garden,
I shake my head. . . . It falls off.

BIRD WITH PAINTED WINGS

Monet whispered softly,
Drowned love
In pools of light.

Picasso shouted nightmares,
Screaming: Climb inside yourself,
There is a madness there.

Braque gave the echo, precisely.

Mondrian exposed squares.

As the Mexicans roared
In the star-torn Indian night,
Fire lifted Paricutin,
Springing red from black earth.

Modigliani, naked, exposed sadness.

Degas exposed angels in ballet skins,
Smoked behind walls of Marseilles' absinthe dens.

Kollwitz served tears in wooden spoons,
Under dark moons, forever sorrowed.

Rousseau shouted poetry
From his window on that mad world.

A burning bird whistled on high:
Eat it all,
Die!

WOULD YOU WEAR MY EYES?

My body is a torn mattress,
Disheveled throbbing place
For the comings and goings
Of loveless transients.
The whole of me
Is an unfurnished room
Filled with dank breath
Escaping in gasps to nowhere.
Before completely objective mirrors
I have shot myself with my eyes,
But death refused my advances.
I have walked on my walls each night
Through strange landscapes in my head.
I have brushed my teeth with orange peel,
Iced with cold blood from the dripping faucets.
My face is covered with maps of dead nations;
My hair is littered with drying ragweed.
Bitter raisins drip haphazardly from my nostrils
While schools of glowing minnows swim from my mouth.
The nipples of my breasts are sun-browned cockleburrs;
Long-forgotten Indian tribes fight battles on my chest
Unaware of the sunken ships rotting in my stomach.
My legs are charred remains of burned cypress trees;
My feet are covered with moss from bayous, flowing
        across my floor.
I can't go out anymore.
I shall sit on my ceiling.
Would you wear my eyes?

TO MY SON PARKER,

ASLEEP IN THE NEXT ROOM

On ochre walls in ice-formed caves shaggy Neanderthals
      marked their place in time.
On germinal trees in equatorial stands embryonic giants
      carved beginnings.
On Tasmanian flatlands mud-clothed first men hacked rock,
      still soft.
On Melanesian mountain peaks barked heads were reared
      in pride and beauty.
On steamy Java's cooling lava stooped humans raised stones
      to altar height.
On newborn China's plain mythless sons of Han acquired
      peaked gods with teak faces.
On holy India's sacred soil future gods carved worshipped
      reflections.
On Coptic Ethiopia's pimple rock pyramid builders tore
      volcanoes from earth.
On death-loving Egypt's godly sands living sacrifices carved
      naked power.
On Sumeria's cliffs speechless artists gouged messages
      to men yet uncreated.
On glorious Assyria's earthen dens art priests chipped
      figures of awe and hidden dimensions.
On splendored Peru's gold-stained body filigreed temples
      were torn from severed hands.
On perfect Greece's bloody sites marble stirred
      under hands of men.
On degenerate Rome's trembling sod imitators sculpted lies
      into beauty.
On slave Europe's prostrate form chained souls shaped free
      men.

On wild America's green torso original men painted
　　　glacial languages.
On cold Arctica's snowy surface leathery men raised totems
　　　in frozen air.
On this shore, you are all men, before, forever, eternally
　　　free in all things.
On this shore, we shall raise our monuments of stones,
　　　of wood, of mud, of color, of labor, of belief, of being,
　　　of life, of love, of self, of man expressed
　　　in self-determined compliance, or willful revolt,
　　　secure in this avowed truth, that no man is our master,
　　　nor can any ever be, at any time in time to come.

CINCOPHRENICPOET

A cincophrenic poet called
a meeting of all five of
him at which four of the
most powerful of him voted
to expel the weakest of him
who didn't dig it, coughing
poetry for revenge, beseech-
ing all horizontal reserves
to cross, spiral, and whirl.

RESPONSE

for Eileen

Sleep, little one, sleep for me,
Sleep the deep sleep of love.
You are loved, awake or dreaming,
You are loved.

Dancing winds will sing for you,
Ancient gods will pray for you,
A poor lost poet will love you,
As stars appear
In the dark
Skies.

WHO HAS SEEN THE WIND?

A Spanish sculptor named Cherino
Has seen the wind.
He says it is shaped like a coil of hardened copper
And spirals into itself and out again,
That it is very heavy
And can break your toe if it falls on your foot.
Be careful when you are moving the wind,
It can put you in the hospital!

ABOMUNIST MANIFESTO

ABOMUNISTS JOIN NOTHING BUT THEIR HANDS OR LEGS,
OR OTHER SAME.

ABOMUNISTS SPIT ANTI-POETRY FOR POETIC REASONS
AND FRINK.

ABOMUNISTS DO NOT LOOK AT PICTURES PAINTED
BY PRESIDENTS AND UNEMPLOYED PRIME MINISTERS.

IN TIMES OF NATIONAL PERIL, ABOMUNISTS, AS REALITY
AMERICANS, STAND READY TO DRINK THEMSELVES
TO DEATH FOR THEIR COUNTRY.

ABOMUNISTS DO NOT FEEL PAIN, NO MATTER HOW MUCH
IT HURTS.

ABOMUNISTS DO NOT USE THE WORD SQUARE EXCEPT WHEN
TALKING TO SQUARES.

ABOMUNISTS READ NEWSPAPERS ONLY TO ASCERTAIN THEIR
ABOMINUBILITY.

ABOMUNISTS NEVER CARRY MORE THAN FIFTY DOLLARS
IN DEBTS ON THEM.

ABOMUNISTS BELIEVE THAT THE SOLUTION OF PROBLEMS
OF RELIGIOUS BIGOTRY IS, TO HAVE A CATHOLIC
CANDIDATE FOR PRESIDENT AND PROTESTANT
CANDIDATE FOR POPE.

ABOMUNISTS DO NOT WRITE FOR MONEY; THEY WRITE
THE MONEY ITSELF.

ABOMUNISTS BELIEVE ONLY WHAT THEY DREAM ONLY
AFTER IT COMES TRUE.

ABOMUNIST CHILDREN MUST BE REARED ABOMUNIBLY.

ABOMUNIST POETS, CONFIDENT THAT THE NEW LITERARY
FORM "FOOT-PRINTISM" HAS FREED THE ARTIST
OF OUTMODED RESTRICTIONS, SUCH AS: THE ABILITY TO
READ AND WRITE, OR THE DESIRE TO COMMUNICATE,
MUST BE PREPARED TO READ THEIR WORK AT DENTAL
COLLEGES, EMBALMING SCHOOLS, HOMES FOR UNWED
MOTHERS, HOMES FOR WED MOTHERS, INSANE ASYLUMS,
USO CANTEENS, KINDERGARTENS, AND COUNTY JAILS.
ABOMUNISTS NEVER COMPROMISE THEIR REJECTIONARY
PHILOSOPHY.

ABOMUNISTS REJECT EVERYTHING EXCEPT SNOWMEN.

SELECTED POEMS FROM

THE ANCIENT RAIN

COUNTESS ERICA BLAISE: CHORUS

Erica Blaise began life with several established truths in her mouth, one was that her father owned three governments and held options on two more. The other was that she was ugly; the aesthetics of her physical make-up had been poorly handled by her maker, and as though in remorse, he had endowed her with all the appetites he had not lavished on the Marquis de Sade. It would not do to bore one with the education and girlhood of an aristocratic European girl, as their lives do not begin until all that is done with, stored with bloomers. Erica, being Countess Blaise, was not allowed to destroy ordinary people, that is, people whose annihilation is handled on a corporate scale. This placed her in the uncomfortable position of having to find two people who were not already spoken for, which is no small task today. Of course, after poking around the flabby corners of humanity, she discovered that the only group still available and in plentiful supply were artists; what's more, they seemed to enjoy it, even demanding wounds that no one was prepared to inflict, as thought their diet was pain—flavored with self-taught self-pity. Erica would not let such hungry people starve, for that would not be civilized. Neither would she turn her back on any who seemed worthy of such historical attentions. She began by collecting major works by artists whose triumphs had placed them outside her game preserve, unearned trophies, but useful lures for less wily game stalking the well-framed jungle. Indiscriminate in her choice of charms to dangle from her social bracelet, she concocted a hodgepodge of self-immolators, unique only for its variety, angelic American girl refugees from Nebraska Victorianism, grateful for the chance to buy Sorbonne dreams in her richly lavendered armpits, English prose writers fleeing Berlitz concentration camps, New York painters pining for one-man shows, which she allowed them to put on so long as they didn't hang pictures, stone cutters, pastel chewers, wire benders, Arab boys with mosaic buttocks, inventors of new artistic movements that lasted one week, unless they became exhausted before the week was out—and fled to Marseilles. Blond German Faustian youth swearing to paint Nietzsche while tripping over borrowed evening gowns amid superman Teutonic giggles, hot-blooded Spaniards who had to be reheated every hour, who painted only their lips, sexy South Americans who slept in boots, and only with each other, explosive Mexicans who would paint only mountains and made love to kill time, Andalusian Gypsies with Flamenco dripping from their fingertips, who would not sin in the same room with a crucifix. African giants hired by the foot, with secret orders to kill Picasso, Italian futurists, who possessed nothing, but a past. Endlessly through the Louis Quinze bush, Erica led that vermilion safari in artistic circles until dizzy with the realization that she was bored, bored open to a new sound, one complete as yet unexplored world, jazz, Africa's other face, stranded—in America, yet to be saved. No Erica anywhere could ignore such a situation; who else can bring the silence so completely? Many. But one must lead.

TELEGRAM TO ALEX/BAGEL SHOP,
NORTH BEACH SF

DEAR ALEX, TOMORROW I AM GOING TO EAT ALL OF THE SUEZ
AND PANAMA CANALS, SO PLEASE DO NOT USE YOUR LIGHT &
GAS AND REFRAIN FROM EYEBALLING FOR TWO SECONDS, WE
HAVE A NEW DEAL FOR CHUCK BAUDELAIRE, THE NEW FRENCH
JUNKIE KID TO PAINT SOME TENDER BATHING SUITS ON MA &
PA KETTLE AND BEARNOG BAROOCK AND CARNAL SPELLMAN
CAN'T COME, SO THERE.

MORNING JOY

Piano buttons, stitched on morning lights.
Jazz wakes with the day,
As I awaken with jazz, love lit the night.
Eyes appear and disappear,
To lead me once more, to a green moon.
Streets paved with opal sadness,
Lead me counterclockwise, to pockets of joy,
And jazz.

[ALL THOSE SHIPS THAT NEVER SAILED]

All those ships that never sailed
The ones with their seacocks open
That were scuttled in their stalls . . .
Today I bring them back
Huge and intransitory
And let them sail
Forever.

All those flowers that you never grew—
   that you wanted to grow
The ones that were plowed under
   ground in the mud—
Today I bring them back
And let you grow them
Forever.

All those wars and truces
Dancing down these years—
All in three flag-swept days
Rejected meaning of God—

My body once covered with beauty
Is now a museum of betrayal.
This part remembered because of that one's touch
This part remembered for that one's kiss—
Today I bring it back
And let you live forever.

I breathe a breathless I love you
And move you
Forever.

Remove the snake from Moses' arm . . .

And someday the Jewish queen will dance
Down the street with the dogs
And make every Jew
Her lover.

[MY MYSTERIES CREATED FOR ME]

MY MYSTERIES CREATED FOR ME
BY GOD ARE UNKNOWN TO
ME, YET I LIVE EACH ONE
PERFECTLY, GOD IS MY GREEN-
EYED ONE, WHOSE POWER IS
ENDLESS. I ASK GOD,
OH GOD . . . TO THE COWARD, GIVE A HORSE
THAT HE MAY FLEE GOD FOREVER,
GIVE CAIN NO FORGIVENESS
FOR WHAT WAS DONE, I ASK GOD,
MY GREEN-EYED ONE, BEFORE THIS
EARTH STOPS SPINNING, THINK OF ME.
REMEMBER, I AM HERE TOO, MY GREEN-
EYED ONE WHOSE POWER IS ENDLESS, AFTER
WHAT WAS DONE TO YOU, WHAT FORGIVENESS . . .
O GOD, MY GREEN-EYED ONE
COME UPON THE EARTH
AND STRIKE THE GLOBE
WITH YOUR WRATH, FOR
WHAT HAS DIED IN THE SUN.
O GOD, MY GREEN-EYED ONE,
PUT YOUR SHARP STARS IN
THE SKY, SEND ORION
THE HUNTER STAR TO HUNT
THE KILLERS OF THE DREAM,
TO HUNT THE SLAYERS OF
THE DIVINE INCUNABULA, O
MY GREEN-EYED ONE, BEFORE THIS EARTH STOPS
SPINNING.

[THE NIGHT THAT LORCA COMES]

THE NIGHT THAT LORCA COMES
SHALL BE A STRANGE NIGHT IN THE
SOUTH, IT SHALL BE THE TIME WHEN NEGROES LEAVE THE
SOUTH
    FOREVER,
GREEN TRAINS SHALL ARRIVE
FROM RED PLANET MARS
CRACKLING BLUENESS SHALL SEND TOOTH-COVERED CARS FOR
THEM
TO LEAVE IN, TO GO INTO
THE NORTH FOREVER, AND I SEE MY LITTLE GIRL MOTHER
AGAIN WITH HER CROSS THAT
IS NOT BURNING, HER SKIRTS
OF BLACK, OF ALL COLORS, HER AURA
OF FAMILIARITY. THE SOUTH SHALL WEEP
BITTER TEARS TO NO AVAIL,
THE NEGROES HAVE GONE
INTO CRACKLING BLUENESS.
CRISPUS ATTUCKS SHALL ARRIVE WITH THE BOSTON
COMMONS, TO TAKE ELISSI LANDI
NORTH, CRISPUS ATTUCKS SHALL
BE LAYING ON BOSTON COMMONS,
ELISSI LANDI SHALL FEEL ALIVE
AGAIN. I SHALL CALL HER NAME
AS SHE STEPS ON TO THE BOSTON
COMMONS, AND FLIES NORTH FOREVER,
LINCOLN SHALL BE THERE,
TO SEE THEM LEAVE THE
SOUTH FOREVER, ELISSI LANDI, SHE WILL BE
GREEN.
THE WHITE SOUTH SHALL GATHER AT
PRESERVATION HALL.

THE POET

FROM A PIT OF BONES
THE HANDS OF CREATION
FORM THE MIND, AND SHAPE
THE BODY IN LESS THAN A SECOND.
   A FISH WITH FROG'S
   EYES,
   CREATION IS PERFECT.
THE POET NAILED TO THE
BONE OF THE WORLD
COMES IN THROUGH A DOOR,
TO LIVE UNTIL
HE DIES,
WHATEVER HAPPENS IN BETWEEN,
IN THE NIGHT OF THE LIVING
DEAD, THE POET REMAINS ALIVE,
   A FISH WITH FROG'S
   EYES,
   CREATION IS PERFECT.
THE POET WALKS ON THE EARTH
AND OBSERVES THE SILENT
SPHINX UPON THE NILE.
THE POET KNOWS HE MUST
WRITE THE TRUTH,
EVEN IF HE IS
KILLED FOR IT, FOR THE
SPHINX CANNOT BE DENIED.
WHENEVER A MAN DENIES IT,
A MAN DIES.
THE POET LIVES IN THE
MIDST OF DEATH
AND SEEKS THE MYSTERY OF
LIFE, A STONE REALITY IN THE

REALM OF SYMBOLS, FANTASY, AND
METAPHOR, FOR REASONS
THAT ARE HIS OWN WHAT IS REAL
IS THE PIT OF BONES HE COMES
FROM,
    A FISH WITH FROG'S
    EYES,
    CREATION IS PERFECT.
SOMEWHERE A BUDDHA SITS IN
SILENCE AND HOLDS THE
POET AND THE WORLD IN
SEPARATE HANDS AND REALIZES HE
IS BORN TO
DIE.
THE BLOOD OF THE POET
MUST FLOW IN HIS POEM,
SO MUCH SO, THAT OTHERS
DEMAND AN EXPLANATION.
THE POET ANSWERS THAT THE
POEM IS NOT TO BE
EXPLAINED. IT IS WHAT IT
IS, THE REALITY OF THE POEM
CANNOT BE DENIED,
    A FISH WITH FROG'S
    EYES,
    CREATION IS PERFECT.
THE POET IS ALONE WITH OTHERS
LIKE HIMSELF. THE PAIN IS BORN
INTO THE POET. HE MUST LIVE
WITH IT. IT IS HIS SOURCE OF
PURITY, SUFFERING HIS
LEGACY,
THE POET HAS TO BE A
STONE.

A FISH WITH FROG'S
EYES,
CREATION IS PERFECT.
WHEN THE POET PROTESTS THE
DEATH HE SEES AROUND
HIM,
THE DEAD WANT HIM SILENCED,
HE DIES LIKE LORCA DID,
YET LORCA SURVIVES IN HIS
POEM, WOVEN INTO THE DEEPS
OF LIFE. THE POET SHOCKS THOSE
AROUND HIM. HE SPEAKS OPENLY
OF WHAT AUTHORITY HAS DEEMED
UNSPEAKABLE, HE BECOMES THE
ENEMY OF AUTHORITY. WHILE THE
POET LIVES, AUTHORITY
DIES. HIS POEM IS
FOREVER.
WHEN THE POET DIES,
A STONE IS PLACED ON
HIS GRAVE, IT IS HIM,
A PIT OF BONES,
CREATION IS PERFECT,
IN THE PIT OF BONES
A SKY OF STARS, A HEAVEN OF
SUNS AND MOONS, AND THE GREAT
SUN IN THE CENTER,
CREATION IS PERFECT.
A MASK CREATED IN THE PIT
IS THE IMAGE OF THE POET.
THE IMAGE OF THE POET
IS A
SECRET.
A FISH WITH FROG'S

EYES,
CREATION IS PERFECT.
I HAVE WALKED IN THIS WORLD
WITH A CLOAK OF DEATH WRAPPED
AROUND ME. I WALKED ALONE, EVERY
KISS WAS A WOUND, EVERY SMILE
A THREAT.
ONE DAY DEATH REMOVED HIS
CAPE FROM AROUND ME,
I UNDERSTOOD WHAT I HAD LIVED
THROUGH. I HAD NO REGRETS,
WHEN THE CLOAK WAS REMOVED,
I WAS IN A PIT OF BONES,
    A FISH WITH FROG'S
    EYES,
    CREATION IS PERFECT.

At the illusion world that has come into existence of world that exists secretly, as meanwhile the humorous Nazis on television will not be as laughable, but be replaced by silent and blank TV screens. At this time, the dead nations of Europe and Asia shall cast up the corpses from the graveyards they have become. But today the Ancient Rain falls, from the far sky. It will be white like the rain that fell on the day Abraham Lincoln died. It shall be red rain like the rain that fell when George Washington abolished monarchy. It shall be blue rain like the rain that fell when John Fitzgerald Kennedy died.

They will see the bleached skeletons that they have become. By then, it shall be too late for them. All the symbols shall return to the realm of the symbolic and reality become the meaning again. In the meantime, masks of life continue to cover the landscape. Now on the landscape of the death earth, the Luftwaffe continues to fly into Volkswagens through the asphalt skies of death.

It shall be black rain like the rain that fell on the day Martin Luther King died. It shall be the Ancient Rain that fell on the day Franklin Delano Roosevelt died. It shall be the Ancient Rain that fell when Nathan Hale died. It shall be the brown rain that fell on the day Crispus Attucks died. It shall be the Ancient Rain that fell on July Fourth, 1776, when America became alive. In America, the Ancient Rain is beginning to fall again. The Ancient Rain falls from a distant secret sky. It shall fall here on America, which alone, remains alive, on this earth of death. The Ancient Rain is supreme and is aware of all things that have ever happened. The Ancient Rain shall be brilliant yellow as it was on the day Custer died. The Ancient Rain is the source of all things, the Ancient Rain knows all secrets, the Ancient Rain illuminates America. The Ancient Rain shall kill genocide.

The Ancient Rain shall bring death to those who love and feel only themselves. The Ancient Rain is all colors, all forms, all shapes, all sizes. The Ancient Rain is a mystery known only to itself. The Ancient Rain filled the seas. The Ancient Rain killed all the dinosaurs and left one dinosaur skeleton to remind the world that the Ancient Rain is falling again.

The Ancient Rain splits nations that have died in the Ancient Rain, nations so that they can see the culture of the living dead they have become, the Ancient Rain is falling on America now. It shall kill D. W. Griffith and the Ku Klux Klan; Hollywood shall die in the Ancient Rain. This nation was born in the Ancient Rain, July 4, 1776. The Ancient Rain shall cause the Continental Congress to be born again.

The Ancient Rain is perfection. The Ancient Rain cured the plague without medicine. The Ancient Rain is vindictive. The Ancient drops are volcanoes and in one moment destroyed Pompeii and brought Caesar down, and now Caesar is fallen. This Roman Empire is no more. The Ancient Rain falls silently and secretly. The Ancient Rain leaves mysteries that remain, and no man can solve. Easter Island is a lonely place.

The Ancient Rain wets people with truth and they expose them-selves to the Ancient Rain. Egypt has a silent sphinx and pyramids made of death chambers so that Egypt remembers the day the Ancient Rain drowned it forever. The mummies no longer speak, but they remember the fury of the Ancient Rain. Their tombs have been sawed in pieces and removed to the graveyard to make way for the pool of Ancient Rain that has taken their place.

The Ancient Rain saw Washington standing at Appomattox and it fell on Lee as he laid down his sword. The Ancient Rain fell on the Confederacy and it was no more.

The Ancient Rain is falling again. The Ancient Rain is falling on the waves of immigrants who fled their homelands to come to this home of Ancient Rain to be free of tyranny and hunger and injustice, and who now refuse to go to school with Crispus Attucks, the Ancient Rain knows they were starving in Europe. The Ancient Rain is falling. It is falling on the N.A.T.O. meetings. It is falling in Red Square. Will there be war or peace? The Ancient Rain knows, but does not say. I make speculations of my own, but I do not discuss them, because the Ancient Rain is falling.

The Ancient Rain is falling in the time of a war crisis, people of Europe profess to want peace, as they prepare day and night for war, with the exception of France and England. They are part of the N.A.T.O. alliance. I believe that Russia wants war. Russia supports any Communist nation to war with weapons and political stances on behalf of any Communist political move. This will eventually lead to war—a war that shall make World War III, the largest war ever.

The Ancient Rain is falling all over America now. The music of the Ancient Rain is heard everywhere. The music is purely American, not European. It is the voice of the American Revolution. It shall play forever. The Ancient Rain is falling in Philadelphia. The bell is tolling. The South cannot hear it. The South hears the Ku Klux Klan, until the bell drowns them out. The Ancient Rain is falling.

The Ancient Rain does what it wants. It does not explain to anyone. The Ancient Rain fell on Hart Crane. He committed suicide in the Gulf of Mexico. Now the Washington Monument is bathed in the celestial lights of the Ancient Rain. The Ancient Rain is falling in America, and all the nations that gather on the East River to try to prevent a star prophecy of 37 million deaths in World War III. They cannot see the Ancient Rain, but live in it, hoping that it does not want war. They would be the victims . . . in

Asia, the Orient, Europe, and in South America. The Ancient Rain will cause them to speak the languages they brought with them. The Ancient Rain did not see them in America when Crispus Attucks was falling before the British guns on the Boston Commons. The Ancient Rain is falling again from the place where the Ancient Rain lives. Alone. The Ancient Rain thinks of Crockett and falls on the Santa Ana Freeway and it becomes a smog source.

The Ancient Rain wets my face and I am freed from hatreds of me that disguise themselves with racist bouquets. The Ancient Rain has moved me to another world, where the people stand still and the streets moved me to destination. I look down on the Earth and see myself wandering in the Ancient Rain, ecstatic, aware that the death I feel around me is in the hands of the Ancient Rain and those who plan death for me and dreams are known to the Ancient Rain . . . silent, humming raindrops of the Ancient Rain.

The Ancient Rain is falling. The Washington
    Monument rumbles.
The Lincoln Memorial is surrounded by stars.
Mount Rushmore stares into every face.
The Continental Congress meets in the home of
    the Ancient Rain.
Nathan Hale stands immaculate at the entrance
    to the Capitol.
Crispus Attucks is taken to school by Thomas
    Jefferson.
Boston is quiet.
The Ancient Rain is falling.

The Ancient Rain is falling everywhere, in Hollywood, only Shirley Temple understands the Ancient Rain and goes to Ghana, Africa, to be ambassador. The Ancient Rain lights up Shirley Temple in the California sky. Meanwhile, in Atlanta, the German U.N. delegation sits comfortably eating in a restaurant that Negro soldiers can't get into, as of some deal between the Germans and the Ku Klux Klan.

The Ancient Rain is falling on the restaurant. The Southern bloc cannot see it.

The Ancient Rain is falling on the intellectuals of America. It illuminates Lorca, the mystery of America shines in the Poet in New York. The Negroes have gone home with Lorca to the heaven of the lady whose train overflows. Heaven.

The Negroes have gone home to be enclosed by the skirts of their little girl mother. Black angels roam the streets of the earth. Make no mistake, they are angels, each angel is Abraham Lincoln, each angel is guarded by Ulysses S. Grant. They are for the death of the Ku Klux Klan at Appomattox. The sword of Lee is no more.

The Daughters of the Confederacy are having a luncheon at the Beverly Hills Hotel in the Savoy room. They are not Daughters of the American Revolution They are not the Mothers of Crispus Attucks. They shall have Baked Alaska for dessert. Their lunch is supervised by a Japanese steward, the French caterer has provided them with special gray napkins.

The voice of Robert E. Lee cannot be heard over the rumbles of Grant's tomb. They leave as they came, the Daughters of the Confederacy, each enclosed in her own Appomattox. Back home they go to Cockalo. Crispus Attucks lying dead on the Boston Commons is the burning of Atlanta by the Union Army. John Brown was God's Angry Man. Crispus Attucks is the black angel of America. Crispus Attucks died first for the American Revolution, on the opening day of American glory. Crispus Attucks does not want a white mother. Crispus Attucks is the Blackstone of the

American Revolution that is known to God. Crispus Attucks is not the son of the South, not the son of Lee, not the son of Jefferson Davis. The South cannot have Attucks for a son. Crispus Attucks is my son, my father, my brother, I am Black.

Crispus Attucks will never fight for Russia. That cannot be said of the Rosenbergs or Alger Hiss or Whittaker Chambers. Crispus Attucks lives in heaven with Nathan Hale. They go to the same school. They do not live in the South.

I see the death some cannot see, because I am a poet spread-eagled on this bone of the world. A war is coming, in many forms. It shall take place. The South must hear Lincoln at Gettysburg, the South shall be forced to admit that we have endured. The black son of the American Revolution is not the son of the South. Crispus Attucks' death does not make him the Black son of the South. So be it. Let the voice out of the whirlwind speak:

> Federico Garcia Lorca wrote:
> Black Man, Black Man, Black Man
> For the mole and the water jet
> Stay out of the cleft.
> Seek out the great sun
> Of the center.
> The great sun gliding
>   over dryads.
> The sun that undoes
>   all the numbers,
> Yet never
>   crossed over a
>   dream.

The great sun gliding over dryads, the sun that undoes all the numbers, yet crossed over a dream. At once I am there at the great sun, feeling the great sun of the center. Hearing the Lorca music in the endless solitude of crackling blueness. I could feel myself a little boy again in crackling blueness, wanting to do what Lorca says in crackling blueness to kiss out my frenzy on bicycle wheels and smash little squares in the flush of a soiled exultation. Federico Garcia Lorca sky, immaculate scoured sky, equaling only itself contained all the distances that Lorca is, that he came from Spain of the Inquisition is no surprise. His poem of solitude walking around Columbia. My first day in crackling blueness, I walked off my ship and rode the subway to Manhattan to visit Grant's tomb and I thought because Lorca said he would let his hair grow long someday crackling blueness would cause my hair to grow long. I decided to move deeper into crackling blueness. When Franco's civil guard killed, from that moment on, I would move deeper in crackling blueness. I kept my secrets. I observed those who read him who were not Negroes and listened to all their misinterpretation of him. I thought of those who had been around him, those that were not Negro and were not in crackling blueness, those that couldn't see his wooden south wind, a tiltin' black slime that tacked down all the boat wrecks, while Saturn delayed all the trains.

I remember the day I went into crackling blueness. His indescribable voice saying Black Man, Black Man, for the mole and the water jet, stay out of the cleft, seek out the great Sun of the Center.

UNCOLLECTED WORKS

Hawk Lawler was born in Kansas City in a charity ward where his father was also born, perhaps in the same bed. His early childhood was that of any Negro child of his town in the nineteen thirties. Regular—attendance at a seedy rundown school, daily salutes to the flag, solemn morning pledges of allegiance, and standard Beard Geographies. A special interest in history led him to build a makeshift log cabin in his back yard in preparation for the presidency, which his father tore down for firewood as soon as he discovered what motivated Hawk. His favorite friends were those with whom he traveled to the relief depot to collect the family ration of potatoes and dried prunes—these boys he trusted; others just happened to be boys, too. In school, he was good in mathematics but hated to do figures on paper. He usually worked out arithmetic problems in his head long before the rest of the class rested their pencils.

He attended church each Sunday at the Rising Sun Baptist Church where he secretly sang hymns in numbers, because he didn't like hearing the same words all the time, yet could offer no resistance to the music. His first personal contact with music as an individual act was when he played triangle in the school band and discovered that when he pinged his instrument at the wrong times he could feel its tingle separate and distinct from the other instruments—at which times he would smile inside his mouth—while apologizing to the leader who was an ex-New Orleans musician that jazz had passed by, yet secretly enjoyed the hard-head. He discovered the saxophone while listening to the band tune up and found that this gilded pipe could play free of the mob; at that instant, he became a saxophone player for life and never touched another triangle. The only possession of which he was proud was an aging Elgin bicycle he received at Christmas from the Afro-American Doll and Toy Fund sponsored by the local Negro paper and provided for by all good white people of the town. It was given to him during a bleak Roosevelt Christmas for winning the school's annual composition contest. His subject was "Why I want to be President," and he was proudest when the bike was presented to him by a snow-bearded colored Santa Claus, whom he recognized as the Mayor's chauffeur. This cherished trophy he surrendered to Horton, son of the family his mother washed for, in return for one battered saxophone which he slept with three nights before feeling intimate enough to try it, and when he did finally find sufficient courage to blow it, his die was cast—he and horn were one, world blotted out.

The only two courses available to him outside of regular studies were the Bible and music, and since he preferred playing the saxophone to being God, his choice was preordained. Before long he was being heard in small local clubs with largely blues clientele. Often experiencing that same feeling about words he had once felt in church, he began to blow numbers; he was fired over and over, yet could not stop blowing numbers. He was hired as second-chair man with the Bat Bowles orchestra, with the provision that he refrain from blowing numbers, which he did, until the band's dilapidated bus pulled up in front of the Theresa Hotel on Harlem's busiest corner, in New York City, where without a word, he picked up his horn case and disembarked. For no reason at all, he walked and wondered. He had never seen so many Negroes at one time in his whole life. He wondered if some big dam had burst in Africa and spilled its contents, or laughed at the crazy thought that they were all white and this was some special holiday when they all wore black and brown faces for some religious Mardi Gras. This speculation was soon replaced by sounds smacking into his eardrums which dispelled any notions of masquerade, causing him to finger his case and peer into doorways for that big hidden jazz womb, oozing blues and down warmth, welcome as new shoes but still emptied of his embryonic numbers.

Strange melodic numbers whose sum total was the blues and so personal no Arab would have acknowledged inventing them—his numbers, each one a fragment of a note. In lieu of finding a room, he found a girl, which was easier in a place where there were more girls than rooms, and while he waited the chance to blow his lover horn again, he blew numbers with his body, which left him sperm-poor and brain-pained, longing to give wind to numbers and breathe life into them. One night his girl-mother-sister-lover-whore had a five-dollar date at one of the better after-hours spots with a leading writer of detective stories, and since this writer was a favorite of his, he went along, taking his horn as always, like some tubular security blanket. Five minutes after he enters the place, God created earth, Christ was born and Gabriel exchanged his trumpet for a saxophone. For there in this headquarters of black revolution sat these long-sought comrades, blowing numbers. Illegal notes floated in air as though they had a right to, floated right into his suddenly blossomed ears, followed him up to the bandstand, crept into his pores as he decased the horn, placed it to his parched lips and sighed, for without willing it they came—numbers, notes, songs, battle cries, laments, jazzy psalms, tribal histories in cubist and surrealist patterns, and an unmistakable call to arms, to jazz, to him, as others put down their horns in silent thanks that he had come, as the drums had promised he would come, come to lead into the unpromised land, littered with pains, odored of death, come to lead, with his pumping, grinning throat. Let us not go into it, we all know he led, though we don't all now how—some of us are more familiar with the intermissions, aware of the passions, privy to the junk, witnesses to the uprising when the handkerchief was cast off; some of us were counters of madhouse excursions, and few of us have withstood the silence, wondering from where it came. Some of us have to know.

DOES THE SECRET MIND WHISPER?

Walk back eating peach seeds after she did that i didn't ask her but i couldn't refuse she seemed so intent then her being only out of jail two years and nothing there to caress her head to give some shelter to the moondrip falling from the evening covering images of those dead soldiers on my lawn in the middle of winter with nothing to cover their sins from the frost dripping from the pocket of those professors sitting in the intersection on their knees praying to the virgin whores to present them with a rubber ball to beat out their father's teeth until he screamed go then he gave them the beautifully wrapped boys to play with until the doctor laughed at his needle sitting there under the moss trees with nothing to do but masturbate and think of the beautiful lesbians in the monsters' arms wishing their father would come and he would kill them and make them brothers so they could play with those dead little boys at the fountain full of that mental wine used on sad holy days also used to chase away all the ghosts hanging around on the corner waiting for haunted girls to pass so they hide in their shoes anxious to throw peach stones at the whorehouse window for the guys to know that it is time for the policemen to come and get laid for all the hard work they are doing to the children to keep the streets safe for the dust to run up those old white steps in the clouds of coughed sorrow to the roof where mag has her goat milking away beneath the star on the left of the television aerial spitting those electric spit balls in everybody's eyes to keep those blue cars rolling along that musclebound street to hell and back in time to eat second hand lobsters from the parole board office down at the local church near the middle of the street just as old mag had that goat killed by raindrop pressures on the headbone most painless way to die since the invention of radio got that italian fellow in trouble up to his neck in messy publicity about politics and the negro vote sticking in his pocket just when jazz jumped out the window and broke the legs of that goddamned old sacrificed goat of mag's lying there waiting for

146

some poor old medicine man to write him a prescription for rock and roll rolling over rocket-burst of clinging forces lashing the reality wall man anti-man again in servile postures grotesque filled skin hunched lanterns cold owl shivering vibrations waiting to wait for waiting death you are now a minor vice your warm lips are far promises forever cold death you are not death yet warmer beds love us human reeling human to you a minor vice life do not leave us till music ends how else living do we know we live or have lived living among endless processions of cocteaus gauchos on bucking motorcycles harsh lights bursting from casual cyclonic winds creeping over strontium landscapes of scorched anatomies of fallen adam birds holding twisted guitars in greek hands caressing us back to old crescent formed wharves of michael faced degenerates whistling over car noises to running statues of fright and can-can memories of fawning buttocks in flickering autumn's bulbs gone before in spiked eyes of lady truck drivers on cracked leg roads to revisited wombs filled with dark brilliant wetness felt in all those sliding eyes glimmering between rumors of truth shouted from sea shell roofs of ochre cardboard huts concealing oracles in furry egyptian cat suits spitting prophecies out of fat stone books from sanded brains of timeless deserts of thebian prostitutes hidden in time beaten minds of made mad translators woven into wrought iron ears and eyes of marble foxes dragging carts of stuffed scented ideas to noiseless suicides behind walls of animated flesh shells while wild visions crawl on airy knees through curly forests of nodding heads strewing bits of shattered images in pointed faces of crepe paper kites flying wildly over petrified idols kneeling on fat walls of glowing flesh in the black rain dripping silently in and out of empty stars drooling over nude bodies of dancing planets celebrating hot birthdays of the sun bannister sliding on twisted bars of light slanting down marble corpse; of twice dead socrates who begat gandhi who begat krishna who begat buddha who begat christ who begat einstein who begat michael who begat melville who begat dostoievski who begat lincoln who begat bessie smith who begat picasso who begat charlie

parker who begat morpheus who begat farnsworth who begat stark-
weather who begat geronimo who begat whitman who begat
hymened women with moist tongues following chinese funerals
escorted by black aeroplanes smokewriting against patent leather
skies beaming soft unbroken rays on glazed foreheads of spoon eyed
painters mourning dead pictures of lost faced girls covered with
tracks of unsuccessful suicides in emptied bays of frantic modern
stonepiles seen plunging into glass faced swamps willed with super-
stitious alligators crawling among monumental statues of sculp-
tured bone lying among busy eight o'clock sidewalks bending under
constant shuffling of hard shoes slipping on petrified tears dropped
from pocked eyesacks of ancient seekers of soft thigh love in navels
of hard breasted adding machine girls in store bought curls wallow-
ing in sipped coffee talking of last night's copulations with certified
public computers and itinerant umbrella peddlers lost in rainless
fogs heel and toe and breast and buttock and crooked neck ballet
dancers seducing male nymphs under cover of secret blankets of
brilliant dust blindly flying through terrified streets of ruined limp-
ing vehicles filled with shaggy mouth youthful gangsters hunting
the human dog with stilettos of fear and dreams of money sex
money cars money suits money shoes money muscles money hous-
es money hair money pearly teeth money pointed shoes money hats
money brains money hate money love twisted into pimp patterns of
money success grasped by money gnarled hands of lanky editorial
writers false teeth credit dentists cheap meat queer butchers hollow
chested bus drivers eye shadow salesgirls all american football busi-
nessmen hollow thigh supermarket clerks money flag makers
money mountain movers money car makers money eyed raw mate-
rial citizens pulped of money landscapes of holy money timemusi-
cal voices of tiny money children cushion noises of disintegration
still heard in dynastic eras of power skeletons stooped in scooped
out offices of company wife husbands custodians of domestic fear
and free terror for still hearted breathers lurking behind neon tomb-
stones singing out corpse voice arias while bristling peaks of

ing with secrets or is it purring at sun caresses does the secret mind whisper to secret organs body message me now i am wanting trapped the new balm tastes of licorice and is shaped like a pickle remember the first steps first fall all the way to a lone floor waking sleeping dust remember the lonesome broomstraws on cold linoleum mesas nimble baby ballet steps pink cuts not quite through the skin deep enough though for a minor cry a quick lip brush tasting like love tingling remember sacred parades of imagined desire remember the girls on the earth one with melted feathers under the crepe de chine curtains the heaven under the tree the world shuts out remember the second breast oh reality leave them alone alone with memory you are too much up on trying to terrify me into existing o reality it is so easy to die in dreams even attend the soul even welcome quiet demise reality don't darken time's corridor or do you too remember hours minutes shoes vests iced glasses tables hands and eyes questions questions turning pages music from warm lips smoky veins on marble tables sinewy wrought iron tongues flickering threats of unholy candles marijuana dreams of perfect purpose remember freckles as we smoked wet fire crackers dreamed rainy day dreams of putting out the sun writing a biography of time on the head of a pin reconstructing her costumes from the shapes of puffs covering our heads with laughing reflecting cracked mirrors oh remember the time on a decadent island ugly whore you mothered then skinny spaghetti slithering from your belly crawling back of my eyes popping into my unprepared skull bathing me in thighs and handfuls of live fat formless bumps little spheres in a new world remember now bury me feet face arms teeth dreams balls swallow me all make me nothing again i want to walk through you on every goddamn street in the world though i see you in dead mind faces of molded brain intellectuals standing on deserted crusty river piers musing on ghostly forms of gone ferries and other sad vehicles of mentality nerve peeled images of transient ecstasies pains of too personal existences private sadnesses hid in smoky dimensions secret pockets in thought cluttered space where love stuffed into unclaimed mountain ranges concealed by sky high forest stretch their necks through newly created clouds of vibrating breath choked from throats of savage inheritors of still rivers flowing serenely from shores of death wheezing civilizations propped on skin shriveled arms of emaciated giants echoing in hollow bodies futile death rattles beneath dark throbbing of burning drums heralding spears of lightning hurled by wealthless savages awakened by the shrill ringing of ceaseless bells tolling the voice of hungry jackals sticking ancient dog faces stolen from egyptian gods into pewter buckets of sour wine drawn from grapes of wrath as bible faced history chanters creep from ice formed caves wearing belts of heat held by hands of cool waiting in nighttime republics long hidden beneath landscapes of memory protected by silk panther stealth satin-finish jacket boys on rows of corners jangling cold dreams in their fist pockets hoarding puberty dreams from crushed breast mothers waiting in kitchen cathedrals for new comings new christ new cancers new drugs new nightmares of female beginnings dying like old dehydrated men sexless at last after nurturing young girl breast in futile hope of love wishing disasters on doomed lipstick daughters new male body queens of bed sweat lovemaking suffering from stretched lips of shame of borrowed contraceptives squirming with giggle noises of skewered pigs among grunts of satisfaction and eternal disease deposited by sexless editorials drummed into defenseless pores and wired into never sleeping ears caught now in moans of fake pleasures murmured over helpless groaning of elastic flesh as oceans of sperm break on reefs of human rocks strewn along shores of time slighted by blinking stars in misty sterile skies silen witnesses to never ending unflinching destruction committed i those thousand names of god who laughs and orders death to laug with him at his withering failures crouched on beds of earth wa and floors of cork were sucking up our conversation as fast as could spit it out through the wordblock o one two why two n number not a symbol a reality oh have you seen my two arms legs two heads two brains two horns on my prickly surly head (

hungry vortexes of crowded eyes loses its shape laughter wears torn aspects memory dredged for forgotten visions offers bitter desire twisted beyond recognition blinded by coppery shadows of old failures concealed inside fake spires of crumbled plastic chapels while silent skull dweller mice fatten on decayed noses of tweedy re-created creatures who shout blasphemy at tigers thrusting ragged dreams through crashed windows sucking fresh jazz into the cages of university pink brain circuses circumspectly shielding their manicured faces from laughing whip eyes of beat oracles doomed to see after bomb visions of eternity imprinted on flattened objective faces of traceless cliffs standing more in unhistoried time unchained winds moving noiselessly through charcoal forest bent staves of burned light darkly illuminating fluted mountains shrouded in flaky smoke warped steel cities filled with a thousand colors of dust web metallic fabric stretched on frames of powderized towers guarding rivers of jellied earth silent lava streets humless unformed shadows heat printed on soft marble canvases gigantic ultimate greek vases posed forever in remembrance of breaths and odors conceived in now time of scraggly haired frightened girls in beer mug barrooms of contemporary revolution on barricades of beds and wine jug bloody fields of screaming no daddy no daddy daddy no daddy away from home terrors of rape me now rape me now babble sounds of hypersensitive talk coming in rhythmic breaths saved from lost evenings memories of paperback conversation with camus and dry old algiers clerks with hidden wagner records stashed in arab oran hotels with whiffs of rimbaud floating in from the holy desert of arab lovers with thousand year eyes and death and no transfiguration not ever but hungry truth picking at cadaverous brainy scarecrows down from the cross forever with handfuls of bent nails screeching martyr cries for hammers of modern romans for veils of sophomore veronicas for tears of convent made marys for vacant shells of unholy sepulchers sealed with blood from anonymous drug stores selling life to death seeking miscellaneous dehumanized beings floating down the night of time in power chariots of glass watched by disinterested clots of self deformed skin and blood with unadjustable souls in torn cellophane garments blue with blues blue like poems everlastingly blue from inner explosions self demolished wrecks proclaiming love on hostile streetcorners spewing wordless gasps spinning themselves into minute histories chapters of crib scenes filled with mother father father sex mother cry fright wet pants screams of delight hate love daddy love mother teacher mother shaped all over mother shapes daddy shapes in clown faces law faces faceless heads in plaster churches of sunday bench kneeling before faceless god and cotton candy sunday night touch swapping of secret feeling of nothing in first disappointments of no more more stop it hurts its raw there we are all raw there from fingernails and rough dreams going up in nervy rockets trailing fire tongues clamped in hot-sharp teeth grinding remembrance to ashes for beds for later flames kindled tall green stink weeds growing like legions of sick candles spurting jets of pepper odors into flaring nostrils lips of salty winds kissing cracked realer flesh caught red eyed with banned imaginations offering solitary thoughts on death and other illegal mysteries carried off in hurricane afternoon's warped glimpses of buried events squeezed from pits of stagnant wax ripped from walls of the mind's eye of goethe taking faust by the hand across dark teutonic landscapes into hitler germanic swamps of twentieth century bosch daylight pushed by blackened wind from bells of spiked trumpets blasting hun fists through the dead body of whore europe's culture as schiller smiled from beethoven's brain trapped in power as certain as timeless karnak booming over luxor's plain to tuscan dusky twilights where torchlit italians carved life in marble mountains ankle deep in severed heads of bloody popes at war with god for rome's remains only to settle for splendored tombs sprung from hands of deathless spirits in tunics of blood and dust crouched in corners of light where creation is master and man does not exist except as tools of art that stern father-mother of souls not of this earth or in it doomed to disappear in traces of works of beauty and love yet reappear in time abstracts of eternal existence pistons of nature doomed to see those dark trees swaying in forests of pain where myshkin begged tortured dostoievski forgiveness in one illuminated flash of remorse for uncommitted sins and deeds left undone cheeks unkissed father unstated love gone ungiven and an idiot's feet were embraced in that maniacal wood where sarah last egyptian first saint mother of all gypsies pumped blood of wild rose into lorca's andalusian veins where federico first sang where mithra in black spanish robes placed her sword in ignacio's groin where sweet lorca weeps bitterly yet lives in the afternoon yet loves in the afternoon that darkly loved wood where all who enter are lost yet live forevermore companion to etruscans and black mountainous shapers of mahogany african breast sucked by old lonely aesthetes looking for lonely women lost on the road to bedrooms of oblivion spreading invisible fingers to steamy corners where athletic gods take all those happy birthday cakes to eat after public showers at baseball games held on heroes' birthdays celebrating lost explorers lost in miserable jungles of old cambodia with many old statues of slant eyed gods and sleepy eyed virgins sunk in muck and lost philosophies dropped by alexander enroute to death in indian jungles and no conquering of asia today baby greek and other traveling civilization salesmen tomorrow more jazz and brand new nook of hebrew tears cast to western skies of gray and other subdued colors mixed by mad mexican painters of old rituals and aztec virgins' breasts spouting rusty blood to cold marble pyramids and jazz dear bitch dear bitch dear bitch dear bitch dear bitch dear bitch where is the robin's nest where is the final sea of flaming waves seeking last shores where the sailor sees gulls and other winged creatures but makes no report for fear of sea god's wrathful eyes filled with painful love and mistaken death you know the score old veteran remover old flickering floozey of destroyed angels and ancient dreams of old embryonic wonder dreams of glory on rounded fields of strange bellies with sandpaper skins bruising tender hands holding other lives cherished from memory of yesterday and today giving communion for all time in new year noises of hopes and forgotten fears blow blow blow blowing through shadow canyons where we stand on wounded feet filled with muddied toys and bones of phantom friends lost in swirling clouds of broken storms flying in heads of adult children left over from illegal xmas forbidden now that space is the thing of momentous impact and drivers of last year's bomb haunting tin littered launching pads enveloped by crushed hopes of unescaped visionaries hung from dying rockers in hidden lunatic afternoons of probe and thrust and naked skies beckoning with ammonia fingers to rootfree wanderers lost to pursuit of womanly earth writhing under rabbit couplings of hurried lovers anxiously disappearing into each other seeking the ultimate bomb shelter deep inside desperate wombs filled with wet butterflies and shells of deserted silkworms gone forever to weave hiroshima's shroud and spin flowers into her burned sod dead of shame and fire great gift of kansas orpheus and god smuggled abroad as co-pilot later seen at survivor's victory celebrations a lone mourner at his family's funeral unnoticed with his eyes of flame amid sheets of swirling vapors of belief in insane embraces with blind animals exhaling hot death breath puffing through laughing playground searing cheeks of children chewing chocolate rockets and no silverbells evermore in times of earache commercials vomited from radioactive radios every minute on the minute sandwiched edgewise between wireless seductions of virginal charity nurses with bargains of old gold and silver and no doctor appendix can't go to menopause party with you must attend lobotomy sale with four out of five leading maniacs on channel last chance for other cathode orgies flowing into wall-to-wall tombs demanding save that poor pregnant wonder horse tragic disguised survivor of apocalypse good i want to count down for the camera and for all clod breasts everywhere in captivity in living rooms dying rooms lonely rooms rooms of hot heads under chrome in beauty parlors whores' rooms in duty palaces good schoolgirls' rooms of friendly masturbations reverberating with father shouts and anthropology dreams of new guinea bush love plucked from savage genitals and men's rooms of leftover sadness of grooved dry whimpering torsos and board rooms where people are split two for one those rooms of frigid supremacy and rooms of hollowed hearts suddenly filling with human mud rising from bowels of blood pumped from painful rooms of rock-eyed poets whispering into their own ears curses too valuable for sealed ear drums of well tailored successes hiding inside scooped paper-filled bellies of concrete giants kneeling at all the proper moments counterpointing fragmented peon noises of it did not happen it did not happen that paul's canary ate radioactive seeds that morning and now only meditates refusing to admit that his song is gone that we sold our blood in hospitals butchers shops only to be busted for dangerous needle marks by a cop who knew god that we stayed in bed all christmas week for fear of offending jesus at gift shops that we were so depressed by the suicide rate we read old newspapers and contemplated suicide it did not happen it cannot happen because it always happens while we hid in buddha's smiling breast drifted to sweeter peaks of self and all seeking those elusive koans hidden in crevices of other navels dug in behind venus mounds of girls who glide onto the spike yet contain no answer but offer only gates of jellied lips opening on other softer queries answered with wet friction and cries of deeper deeper deeper stab me through impaled on that bony question answers fly to the loins and life is stabbed into existence as orgasmic silence bathes the room in peace as questions disappear rolling down ballooning bodies in milky crystals of sex odored sweat drowning interhooked feet in pools of giving taking giving never what is asked taking many times more until empty of self free of self until possessor of self in this time of sour bees and rancid honey we are not flowers no lilies grow in our eyebrows and our skulls are potential ash trays for those fires smoth-ered in cores of men smoldering hot coals fuming to burst into flame yet we shall stand naked and cool them with angry love songs.

J'ACCUSE

The city is a jealous bitch,
    hardening her sidewalks when she sees us
        walking toward the moon,
            satirically echoing our hesitant steps.

The city is a jealous bitch,
    lighting all the doorways we need,
        to dig into each other's mouth and hair,
            sadistically sowing bus stops in our path.

The city is a jealous bitch,
    purposely growing skyscraping office buildings
        on the vacant lots in which we offered each other
            as one singular tribute, to our personal star.

The city is a jealous bitch,
    lighting the night with morning,
        leaving us writhing with unexploded atoms
            whirling in our loins.

The beautiful city is a jealous bitch.

NO MORE JAZZ AT ALCATRAZ

No more jazz
At Alcatraz
No more piano
for Lucky Luciano
No more trombone
for Al Capone
No more jazz
at Alcatraz
No more cello
for Frank Costello
No more screeching of the
Seagulls
As they line up for
Chow
No more jazz
At Alcatraz

from *Beatitude*

MONGOLIAN SUNSET IN GOBI DESERT

The road
It takes you
And it slows you down.

Oh Cleo. She knew
The road in California.
When Autumn; the Spring
She knew
Cities, lights, music
And the Dharma Bums.

Anthony knew too.
What was yesterday's
Victory
Today's agony.

Cleo and Anthony in the
Arkansas Farm watchin'
The Big Trees grow.

Note: In 1980, Bob dropped this one on the floor of Curley's, an unpretentious
North Beach diner, where for years Bob could be found in the early morning having
breakfast.

PEACE BE WITH YOU

THE GUNS OF WAR ARE SILENCED,
IT IS NOT AS IT WAS
THE CROWD DOES NOT DEMAND BLOOD.
PEACE IS NOT A CASTLE IN SCOTLAND,
IT IS NOT THE FIRST TEXAS BANK,
IT IS NOT THE GETTY EAR.
A CRY FOR PEACE IS HEARD AT BREST-LITOVSK,
THE PAVILION RESPONDS,
WITH THE MUZZLING OF THE CANNON,
IT IS NO LONGER HEROIC
TO WALK INTO THE GUNS,
THE MEN WHO DIED IN PREVIOUS WARS
HAVE BECOME PRESIDENTS & POPES
AND PRINCES OF THE LAND.
NOW THEY WANT A PEACE
THAT CAN BE THE MEANING OF THE CROWN,
IN KOREA AFTER THE KILLING,
THIMINYAYA DEFINED THE PEACE,
PEACE IS THE TRUTH,
THE WORLD MUST EITHER RESPOND TO IT
OR SPONSOR THE BLOODLETTING THAT WAR IS.
I HAVE BEEN IN THE WARS OF THE PAST,
THEY ARE MY MEMORIES OF MY YOUTH,
SICILY, NORTH AFRICA, SOUTH AMERICA,
EGYPT, INDIA, EUROPE,
I KNOW THE KILLING FIRST HAND.
I STAND FOR PEACE
I KNOW WHAT IS HAPPENING AT THE PENTAGON,
WAR CANNOT STOP IT,
NOTHING CAN STOP IT.
I AM A BAGEL SHOP PERSON,

YET I SPEAK FOR PEACE IN THE COUNTRY,
IN THE CITY,
ALL OVER.
SOMETIMES A FAKE CALL FOR PEACE LURES THE WORLD TO
WAR,
AS CHAMBERLAIN WITH HIS
"PEACE IN OUR TIME"
SENT THE WORLD REELING INTO WORLD WAR TWO.
BUT THIS IS NOT IT,
THIS IS A MESSAGE
FROM THE CLOUDS,
FROM THE STARS
FROM THE SKY
PEACE.
THIS IS NOT THE END
A THOUSAND MEN LAY DOWN THEIR GUNS,
UNTIL THE PEACE IS AN ORDER
SO MANY DEAD WHO DID NOT SEE
THE VINDICTIVE BUDDHA,
THIS IS THE PLACE THAT WE HAVE TO COME TO,
TO ANSWER FOR ALL THE QUESTIONS WE HAVE ASKED,
THIS IS THE PLACE
AND, THE TIME.

Note: Written on Old Cazadero Road in the Russian River area of northern California, October 30, 1983.

A BUDDHIST EXPERIENCE

A BUDDHIST EXPERIENCE
CANNOT GIVE IT A NAME OR SHAPE,
MIGHT SEEK TO FIND A CONTEXT
TO UNDERSTAND THE LANGUAGE BEING USED,
HISTORICAL, YES,
ALSO SOMETHING ELSE,
HOW PEOPLE EMERGE FROM THE GROUP,
COMPLETE, INDIVIDUAL,
EACH RESPONDING TO SOME HIGHER STONE
OF ORDER UNCHALLENGED
IN THE SEARCH FOR MEANING,
IN REACHING FOR THE PURE RELATION,
TO INTERPRET LIFE AND BY THAT INTERPRETATION
TO LIVE MORE DEEPLY IN ZEN,
ZEN OF THE REAL RED BONE,
LIKE COLTRANE,
WHO IS PLAYING THE SAXOPHONE,
SPEAKING OF LIFE AND DEATH
AND WHAT LIES IN BETWEEN,
THE BALLOONS RISING UP
SEEM TO TAKE THE POET TO THE SKY,
PERHAPS THE SAME SKY AS THE LITTLE FRENCH BOY,
THEY SAILED INTO THE HEAVENS,
NOW THE INYO MOUNTAINS SPEAK THEIR MEANING,
I AM THE SKY ROCK
THE PLUNGING ROCK,
WAITING TO BE SURROUNDED BY CLOUDS,
TO ILLUMINATE THE ANGELS PATROLLING THE EARTH,
THE HEAVENLY BRIGADE MOVING MYSTERIOUSLY
THROUGH EVERYTHING,
SHOULD I SPEAK TO THEM?

I DO.
I ASK THEM FOR A LIFE THAT CAN BE LIVED IN HEAVEN
WHILE BEING LIVED ON THE EARTH,
I ASK THEM TO MAKE THIS POSSIBLE,
THEY SPEAK OF THIS EARTHLY LIFE
AS A TRANSITION TO A DIFFERENT EXPERIENCE,
SOME PLACE ELSE,
PEOPLE SEEM TO HAVE PERSONAL REASONS FOR WHATEVER THEY
DO
I MUST FIND MY MOTIVES.

THE TRIP, DHARMA TRIP, SANGHA TRIP

IS A DELIBERATE ATTEMPT
TO REBUILD A LIFE,
SEEMS TO BE DEMOLISHED
LIKE AN OLD BUILDING
NOBODY WANTS TO LIVE IN
YET STANDS HOPEFULLY.
SOMETHING MORE THAN MEMORY
IS NEEDED,
WORDS ARE NOT A SOLUTION,
SOMETIMES THEY ARE A PROBLEM,
BUT THE PEAK MUST BE REACHED,

THE ROAD GOES ONLY TO THE TOP OF THE MOUNTAIN,
SEEMS THERE IS NO PLACE ELSE TO GO
LIFE ON A MOUNTAINTOP
WITH SKY ALL AROUND,
A VIEW OF EVERYTHING SPREADING OUT
BEFORE THE EYES,
REPLACING WORDS WITH IMAGES.

Note: Bob's last poem, Chinese New Year, 1985. Written after Philip Whalen visited him and after a trip to the Dharma Sangha in Santa Fe, New Mexico.

Bibliography

WORKS BY BOB KAUFMAN:

Abomunist Manifesto (broadside) (San Francisco: City Lights, 1959).

The Ancient Rain (New York: New Directions, 1981).

Does the Secret Mind Whisper? (broadside) (San Francisco: City Lights, 1960).

Golden Sardine (San Francisco: City Lights, 1967).

Second April (broadside) (San Francisco: City Lights, 1959).

Solitudes Crowded with Loneliness (New York: New Directions, 1965).

WORKS WHICH INCLUDE CONTRIBUTIONS BY BOB KAUFMAN:

Black American Literature, ed. Ruth Miller (New York: Macmillan, 1971).

California Bicentennial Poets Anthology, ed. A.D. Winans (San Francisco: Second Coming, 1976).

The New Black Poetry, ed. Clarence Major (New York: International Publishers, 1969).

New Black Voices, ed. Abraham Chapman (New York: Mentor, 1972).

La Poesie de la Beat Generation (Paris: DeNoel, 1960).

The Poetry in Black America (New York: Harper & Row, 1973).

Three Authors. (Paris: L'Herne, 1969).

BIOGRAPHICAL SOURCES ON BOB KAUFMAN:

Abbott, Steve. "Bob Kaufman: Hidden Master of the Beats," in *View Askew: Postmodern Investigation* (San Francisco: Androgyne, 1989), 128-141.

Cherkovski, Neeli. "Celebrating Second April: Bob Kaufman," in *Whitman's Wild Children* (Los Angeles: Lapis, 1988), 101-121.

Clay, Mel. *Jazz—Jail and God* (San Francisco: Androgyne, 1987).

Foye, Raymond. "Private Sadness/ Notes on the Poetry of Bob Kaufman," in *Beatitude 29* (San Francisco: North Beach, 1979), 71-83.

Hirschman, Jack, ed. *Would You Wear My Eyes?: A Tribute to Bob Kaufman* (San Francisco: The Bob Kaufman Collective, 1989).

Kaufman, Eileen. "Laughter Sounds Orange at Night," in *The Beat Vision* (New York: Paragon House, 1987), 258-267.

Rigney, Francis. *The Real Bohemia* (New York: Basic Books, 1961).

Starer, Jacqueline. *Les Ecrivains Beats et le Voyage* (Paris: Didier, 1977).

Winans, A.D. "Bob Kaufman," in *Dictionary of Literary Biography, Vol. 16, The Beats: Literary Bohemians in Postwar America*, (Detroit: Gale Research, 1983), 1, 275-278.

Note: Bob Kaufman appears thinly disguised as "Chuck Berman" in Jack Kerouac's novel *Desolation Angels* (New York: Coward, McCann & Geoghegan, 1965).

FILMS, RADIO & TELEVISION PROGRAMS THAT FEATURE BOB KAUFMAN:

Dee, Ruby, and Ossie Davis, "Coming from Bob Kaufman, Poet," television program for PBS, 1972.

Felver, Chris, and Gerald Nicosia. "West Coast: Beat and Beyond," Sixty-minute video program shown on KQED Channel 9, San Francisco, 1984.

Henderson, David. Four-hour program for KPFA-FM radio, Berkeley, 1987-1988.

Kesey, Ken. "Ken Kesey's First Poetic Hoo Haw," video of Bob Kaufman reading his poetry in Eugene, Oregon, 1976.

Rice, Ron. *The Flower Thief*, film, 1959.

Tynan, Kenneth. *Dissent in the Arts in America*, film, 1959.